# DEATH AND

## YARROW YES WOODS

This is an Inside the Castle publication of

**DEATH AND**

by
Yarrow Yes Woods, ©'d in 2023
the 46th publication of literature in the expanded field
as curated from the geographic center of the United States
Lawrence, Kansas

This book is designed by John Trefry and typeset primarily
in Franklin Gothic, a grotesque typeface designed by Morris
Fuller Benton and named in honor of Benjamin Franklin
who, at age 22, wrote his own epitaph: *The Body of B.
Franklin Printer; Like the Cover of an old Book, Its Contents
torn out, And stript of its Lettering and Gilding, Lies here,
Food for Worms. But the Work shall not be wholly lost: For
it will, as he believ'd, appear once more, In a new & more
perfect Edition, Corrected and Amended By the Author.*
Background texts are set in **Abril Fatface**.

re untroubled descent into madness the
ntasy became necessary to survive, she sews
gether several long swaths of heavy fabric
nd hangs them over the years. between them
e dust we touch the Shop-Vac to, modified
il and beak to brush. when the cloth waves
makes blue notes on the carpet. outside the
rdinals and blue jays. the robins. an old green
ding lawn mower stuck up a tree. when it is
t the fabric multiplies to keep the cool air in
hen it is cold, the fabric multiplies to keep the
ld out. in between the pollen and noise, the
orms the rain the wind shake the old roof
t a minute to spare the crystal angel trinket
ve turned in the mirrors above the mantle
he mantle scorched the days forget when
e vacuum caught the cinders the callused
irror the candles lit blackening the walls wax
ticulating the sound of possibility. someone
uld have broken in the alarm systems have
oubled and signs thereof tripled. fantasy is the
eginning of the most powerful magic she show
e a photo of a man and tells me his life His lif

he threats grow in specificity. Should I b
larmed he says when we return home Lov
s like that sometimes and why we can't tak
he car: my father has been loosening the
ugnuts and cutting the brake cables. oh. it
hat animals breed more dangerous animals
ny teeth sharpen themselves and my tongu
uts itself like grass. It's all about power fo
he thread and needle basket opens without
atch and the alcohol won't swab for sanitatio
he closer we get the more apparent the
ack of touch and when we touch its pain
verwhelming. Why should the cops be calle
n the pre-teen and barely teenage siblings
The attic is so hot and humid and the asbesto
To access the attic fans one must unscrew th
ld, heavy, wooden covers. I stand on the old re
airdressing stool and brace myself. If it is
m, it is a good time to call the police again. Th
hreats amass and the children take turns bein
hoved into a corner and kneed in the groin an
it in the face with the rings and bony par
f a hand. The pigs arrive just as everyone h

A major problem with this text is that Death is a name
For my lover of years & my lover of months & my dad
& my best friend trans-dad/trans-twin & my cousin & my
Five aunts the queer ones & the queer ones who are
Straight & my sibling & my mom & who all i try to care for
As any girl might, as any devoted to the one bloody truth thin-
King̶ly friends are family *Are What?* i have to lose & mort-
Gage & down payment & buy the hellscape farmboy a
Drink at the bar before he tries to do the same to you.

Problem two involves my father who met Death with a car and
A garage right? Oh so right. i reshingled the roof. made sure it
Wouldn't leak. Sealed tight. 10 Years before! and 100 Years before it's true
When he first said he would kill himself, he said he failed as a father
because he couldn't afford it. but it was the medical debt from surviving
Hepatitis C and a wealth of other horrors, still in calling him every week

or dress̶ ███████ a girl or every little perversion or not saying the exact right word/spell
or really ̶o̶u̶t̶ keeping the garage/shed from falling apart
i made his Death easier. *it's not true*. Death is so easy for me. He kissed
on the first day and on the second, They dropped Their panties, sure
i too am a cumslut for Death is this? The Third Body problem? Death and i work then come
home
in a gig[olo] economy. three jobs four jobs five jobs yes! part-time full-time
beneficiaries on my wall a painting the painter my father loved gave me

says, translated, *Life is a game and Death is always dancing*. His
[My father's] letters are missing. suicide notes i mean. when i write them
mine[field day] with a program on my phone, letter by letter, mistake by mistake

until i can't write another one [spring summer winter fall sleep]
too many people to write to the Death i adore and the ones i can't
help [but to imagine] have to find a way to stay alive [like father like s–]

Are they called pigs because they sometim[es]
savage their young? Sows or first-tim[e]
farrowers only ever do this in high-stre[ss]
environments, say, like in crates or pins
loose-d... ...s... ...grow to slaughte[r]
A lead... ...questions whether you[r]
gilts or... ...have been able to for[m]
sound... ...experience normal birthi[ng]
practic... ...ed... Savaging is a rejection
their fun... ...shortened lifetim[e]
of torture... don't know... n't think anyo[ne]
could say... it would have to be something
would consider. Some studies have suggest[ed]
that pigs allowed to raise each other in a fre[e]
roaming environment might not kill and e[at]
their newborn babes, but there are questio[ns]
about how economically feasible this is. wh[en]
i was small, i believed in pigs eating each oth[er]
this savaging to be the most visceral traitoro[us]
act—why officers of the law got that name—b[ut]
now i know something of savagery, and i kn[ow]
it to be the most divine, the most devout and
theirletter, theysay "...devouring--onlybecau[se]

so i write them like this:

Delete line /break/ page /break/ fall /break/ neck /break
/ Bread /break fast break coffee break bed break spring
Break breach bREAK Eabrkea bkhdssasjl btrrwaaj br
Eak out capitalize break capitalize break lower break
Case break end quote break file break safe offline mode
Break line break off break communication break
Break open break file break word break bank break
Break type break capitalize e break capitolize k
Back break space break backspace backs /break/ pace
Break insert break page break insert break image
Break insert break character break down break down
Break underline break draw break S break H break E
br  ea k the obsession with Death with opening the window
bre - -a-k the train tracks one step away break wait from not
br__k a stream a bobblehead a bauble one more night break coping mechanism
break comfort in the yhought hours and hours
break in the typ[o-graph!]ical error message

consuming
you whole is
the only way
I can resolve

I.

So we were born so
we brought ourselves to Listen to
a hand on our asses

the screaming took a long time
to get back to us
we get it already   :    the tablecloth is not a dress

the glass pink rose has no stem
or dewy beetle pressed
into grass  What becomes

fork when placed to your lips
& wht bcms shovel
You were asked all the wrong questions
at the hospital at the [operating/dinner] table

but You cme anyweigh to
thhhh right place
where the cottonmouth swims    [F O R M AL DE H I D E
to fix t he tissue]

if you Spin The Jar
n n               on the shelf
all the signs say DON'T Touch

and we don't
we don't

only by night?
Only by accident

stuffing panties  pull them out
cloud   sinks    threaded silk

Imitation No.
Means   No
one got boiled    no worm anyway        alive
to become        placeholder

for the internal either

I LOVE IT
or
   or
i don't mind

tearing
some
a LITTLE    t[h]read on me
Needlepoint'ST   ITCH

s_wing then s_wing   not too tight

makes room
for growth
turn

he cognitive dissonance I feel when caug between my hunger and my utter satisfaction le pours the water into the decanter to make red jewel, sure a ruby it's the only one i know golden hour. Because I call them by their on rightful name, is an expectation that the tig circles of bite marks are to protect me? Fro he satiation from the savaging of our ow desires? And my heart diluted into water to fee he plants on the long windowsill? This is for the safety? That can't be right but it is true. The co concrete is painted forest green when I retur Should it stain my bare feet?  The oxygen t nourishing pleasure returning with th sunlight. i return to my deepest terror with second armor. So the wound opens and appea as shadow, the liquid red crowding out yello nd white rose petal. So the skin hardens a softens. Restoration is not made toward replic Not a seamless overlapping. i write a letter he home and the fear ever new inside whe always am. Am i wrong to say this again? make a wall is to make the idea of an entran

yellow paper

yourself      inside         out
burn
to powder    Death says    If it's real

silk    smells like burning hair
no. 7


not 2 or 3

how many gorgeous days do you time for

i can't count
that high                              without breaking

The more impenetrable the wall, the graver the idea of encroachment.

fill in the blank
when i lower case the capital
it refuses    The Type    a [pay] stub[ble/born]
backspace    REENTER    backspace backspace
REENTER      back space RE ENT ER abc kps ace
autocomplete   so   handy   so   man u al   Read: all
directions before beginning      tips & tricks
FAQ'S   is this ok      do you want breakfast   are you alright
if i step out for a second   will you want a blanket
to uncover   the first lie where do you go
when you're ending   [today beneath the crick]   trimble
[ ]ath[ ] beginning make small   talk   [ ]ell of yr fac[ ]
use the letter   bank !
[T B H] rearrange me  [SH E] it doesn't sssk [P I L E]  some
things
Grow Large      get with the program    auto
Correct    by hand   yr answers

earlier – cognate – courtesan  [failed]

hypocotyl        the sun came out
                 the moon came OuT
all day luckleless day

then i throw it away

        n    n    n     nn    oo oooo  o ooo   o

     O O  O    N    NNNN    NNNNNN

brick. It can be fluid like water, or bloo
or a the footfall dampening of fabric. So the
i thought everyone else thought pigs we
just dirty, wallowing in filth and flood. A
then I think captivity. And of a monke
wrench on the table near the woman
hand, the broken wine glass stem and th
sharp wire of a guitar string beside the chil
Now i see that the pigs got their name fro
sniffing around, the ways the animals d
And they do. place their snouts to th
fabric, they put their breath ravenou
only vaguely conscious searching
every bend and every swale. They ro
through ever corner of the woman
face, nothing of savagery, nothing
the devout or the divine in their gruntin
nothing of protection and nothing
serving in their glut, and they open the
drooling, half-bearded maws and ea
everything they touch. Everything th
touch unravels like a twirl of entra

Death tells me I have to leave??
hell it's more complicated than that
what the fuck am i supposed
to say ?? Who am i Protecting?
The LAND??!! THE WATER ?!?
THE YET FERTILE WOMB OF
THE OCEAN IS IT STRAINING
NOW AGAINST THE HORIZON

LEGAL    TENDER
BITCH            BUILD ME
U  GUESSED IT      A FIRE
        Hazard : to
WRITE              Draw The Water
ON        Make Your Mark   xxx
          the line gets darker
THE MONEY

To prove false : counterfeit
Death used to be a Horsegirl

Tonight They are in my arms

[if ... may turn to page 27
and begin your study there]

The person who [REDACTED] me
when i was too young to remember??
That i would stand in the shower
at 4 5 and 6 and check my asshole
to see if i was ready to be fucked??

beneath the covers two bodies and one of them i say is mine. i say Yr mine to the other body and the other body understands. sleeping together little deaths how i loathe them? but i'm misquoting the nightmare    tonight  four hours my voice rasps    but earlier    i said "speaking of radical destruction: break [all over] me" & "lay waste to meeeee" & the other body responded with a poem. a line from that poem "Once you blur the distinction between equal and equivocal, space is interrupted and disappears in subcutaneous shivers." all my metaphors for sex involve dissolution. u n i versal solvent. the other body gets  so wet flooded  my house  my foundation melts. "im a puddle" the other body says in a text but i know they are an ocean (why else would i say break): "tonight let's practice erosion / it's finally my turn as the wind" but wind carries the sediment   the soil   the salt   that does the work. the wind a vessel    for other smaller bodies & these bodies get no nominal credit. i take credit    for what?

my body does to this other body. call it a kink because the string was knotted already. *to bend at the knees* kick & kick like a hanging body. call the neck a curl in the rope. that paroxysm of DIE IN TH[E]Y LAP. in a 90's film the villain threatens *i can make you laugh* but we all know he    because laughter    means *as close to Death as one can get* & so does   Beaten Within    an inch of our lives    swimming    melting makes a body [its limits] harder to define. measure the shoreline. measure a cloud. when it rains. measure the size of your mouth. without teeth now. sometimes i imagine silly things like the other body tearing open my side with their fingers. splitting me from hip to shoulder. silly because i ???? from kissing the other body on the bed, then more until i push the other body from my body and say Fuck You sometimes. You have to stop touching me, but my body doesn't listen. the fan the blanket on my leg hair   its cool   the wet spots on the bed against every footstep outside the door creaking on the stairs there are  cars  outside with bodies in them and the lights on the window make me shake so    i have to hold it. i learned to palm pain this way, a needle through my ear through pinched arm torture videos snuff films accidental deaths (one i remember: a body  pushes

there are many horrors that you
don't deserve to know, reader
lover, friend, enemy combatant
unintended casualty of casual life
missile over the silk mug
surveillance resume over live
feed ferally burnt to plastic
goddess... plush pillow
pushing... million to
alert the homeowner distant
murder of cow delivery
driver reversing into a delivery
bicyclist sophist skulduggery
Fifth daughter of the God Wolf,
First song of the God-filled gut
Allium Sweet Potato Shrub;
Gland Sycamore Rain summer
Pillbug Maple Seed Catalpa Pods
Do you believe my origin story
is any different from yours?

# Do you believe my origin story is any different from yours ?

a tall metal lattice structure with wheels across a street then the body falls to the ground and does not move after. comments on the video say the structure touched an electrical wire. the body does not move but the tall lattice rolls away. this   a .gif  so it recurs: pushing the cart, falling to the ground, silent the whole time, but more silent when the body stops moving) & opening   making with shaving-razorblades new mouths on my stomach n chest that breathed when i did   tore horizons from the scabs messy sunsets   in the skin giving myself too much of it. isopropanol poured into each gap. estuaries  bringing  my body  outside itself  when  dams break i try to teach myself to take pleasure the same, small steady breaths each flex flux "dust me up" of my core and legs too tightening but sometimes the ecstasy is too loud or bright n i lose my body  n   every sense. no light now. sparkles. glitter terrible world i lean into of  the dark i was always scared of. n this height too. i look down inward n vertigo oh sweet one come back to me, terminal

velocity occurs because the wind resists the body. the body might erode completely   if falling for long enough.  the shape changes too quickly to mark. well. in dead space, this is no problem. no problem at all you can accelerate for infinity. or maybe until the speed of light when you become pure energy. tonight i do & i have left   becoming  ageless  faceless when i return   nothing is different  except in the morning  my hair lingers on my lips and it is lightning on the walk to the bus   sometimes   the shift of my bandana around my neck  bruised  sometimes it's the light reflecting off my hand  my tongue caught between my teeth when the bus passes under a bridge   potholes beneath the wheels  specters of the other body  of the other night   rapping on my windows    sometimes    it's just the wind

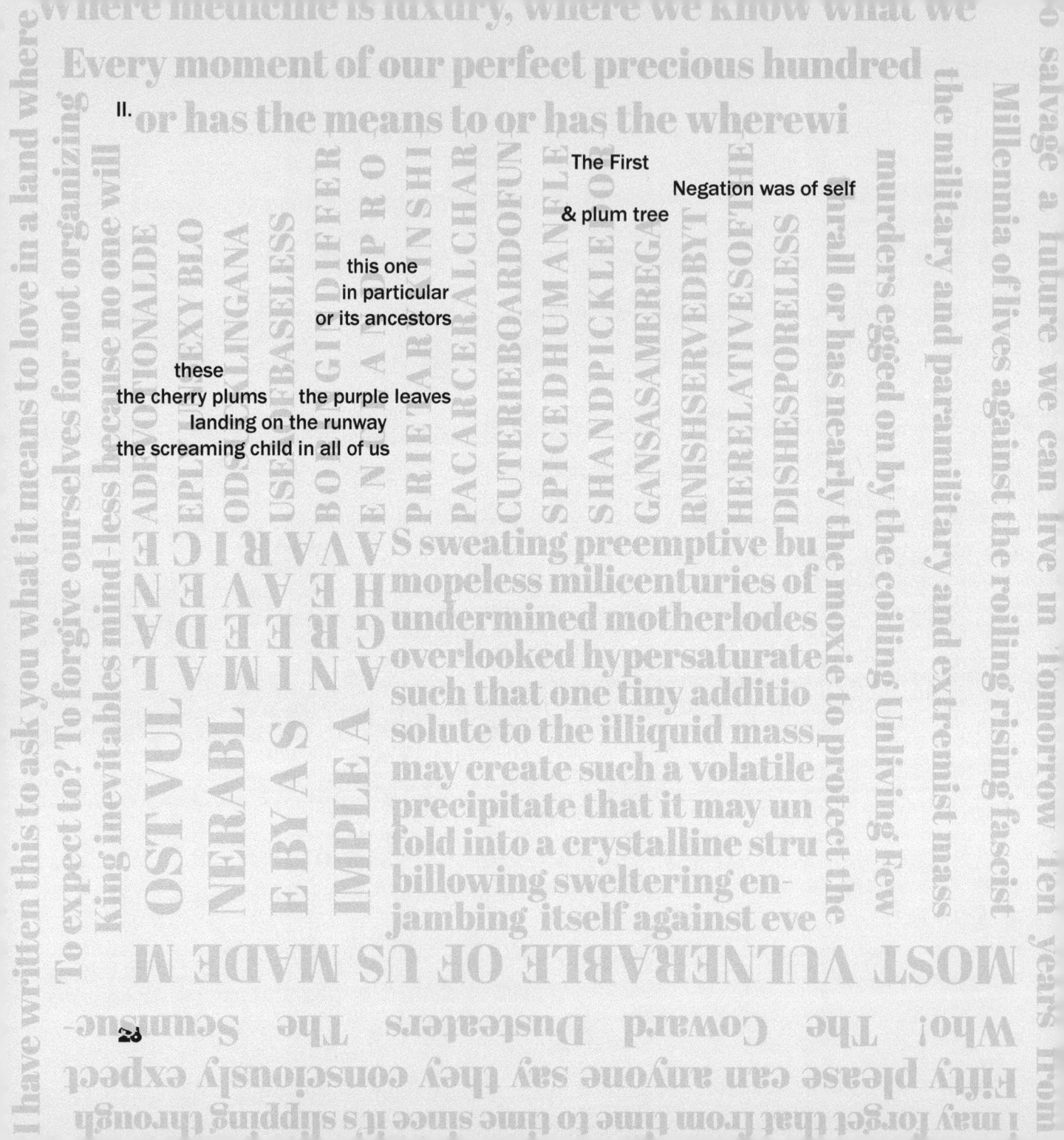

II. or has the means to or has the wherewi

The First
Negation was of self
& plum tree

this one
in particular
or its ancestors

these
the cherry plums      the purple leaves
landing on the runway
the screaming child in all of us

S sweating preemptive bu
mopeless milicenturies of
undermined motherlodes
overlooked hypersaturate
such that one tiny additio
solute to the illiquid mass
may create such a volatile
precipitate that it may un
fold into a crystalline stru
billowing sweltering en-
jambing itself against eve

MOST VULNERABLE OF US MADE M

swallowing all in its tongueless

path to fullness????? a drop

of forever, distilled and

distilled inmortality into

the American Family are

you without sin without Fear

let you cast the first stone

in bronze then as a memoria

to its dying shape, cast the

dirt into sand into rock once

more POUR IT INTO YOUR

PRECIOUS EVERYSONG MOUTH

 i am all ghost at work
not the [house/dick] cleaning jobs

trying to remember my training
i consult my notes
from the Whole Foods orientation class

GREET EVERYONE WITHIN
FIVE SECONDS
SCROLL
WASH YOUR HANDS
ASK THEM WHAT THEIR STORY IS
THEIR STORY TELLS YOU WHAT TO SELL
CHANGE GLOVES
THE WORD 'NATURAL' IS NOT DEFINED BY ANYBODY
THE WORD 'NATURAL' DOESN'T ACTUALLY MEAN
'ANYTHING'
ASK
IF YOU DON'T KNOW
SIDESELL
UPSELL
CHANGE THE CHANNEL TO SOMETHING WE ALL CAN ENJOY
A DISNEY FILM SPORTS A COMEDY MAYBE NICE VISUALS
CHANGE YOUR GLOVES
JAMES MACKEY & JEFF BEZOS
COUGH INTO YOUR SLEEVE
WASH YOUR HANDS

| | |
|---|---|
| SOAP DOWN | WIPE |
| WATER | WIPE |
| SANITIZE | WIPE |

BE ENRICHED
PACK MEAT
BRIDGE FAILURE TO REPAIR
ALL THE MOUTH
FALL & FALLOW
LOL LOL
THINK THESE AND NOT THOSE
WASH YOUR HANDS BEFORE YOU DO ANYTHING
WET FINGERS
DON'T FIT
INTO GLOVES

AND GULP, GULP FOR ME
AS IT TUMBLES WET DOWN
INTO YOUR BOWELS BURROWS
INTO YOUR NARROWS SLINGING
SAVOR AND SUCCOR AND WEARY
IS THIS THE NEGATIVE
CAPABILITY
WE SHOULD BE SEEKING

28

o the stone will praise you, p
ur defiance, your courage, t
nceremonious tones your tend
ellow as you unfold yourself
nother day of refusing to dre
efusing to eat, refusing to ta
leasure, but merely acceptin
eathly white supremacy-base
ther, perfect oval worm in a
ink harness perfecting its wh
nd its kiss, perfecting its slu
ear, the pity you feel have yo
elt??? The mere sense of its
ain, now your pain, gumchew
ch skin strip, feeding off ev
ou can manage to inhale, pre
ored people pretending to lo
apeless the words unjawed a
ading from the most settling
eryman, tuned to the perils
alaise of security, guilt of s

**TREAT ALL BLOOD AND FLUID AS IF THEY HAVE—ARE CONTAMINATED**

Happens to be cleaned

Whirlygig-blizzard-wielding Death rays I can't keep my hands off you
Summers'tutting can't keep my clothes on... apparently

what i came to do...i said Unbidden...to tell about a mind
on my knee

the manoeuvres (cure for poetry)
to cry on the bus

i drink a pint

then i buy another

the thing about pints

(No no no) one looks good

i pretend... tuned to the perils of wealth

he says

I'm in the dark hole

Another says I'm just a good guy looking for a good woman

i tell him i need first class and twelve grand a day

think about it

Gods i reach for it off your cheek and surprise
It has disappeared!! Disappeared

3)

*Nothing lasts he says*
*Aw baby even*
*diamonds erode in the ocean*

bringing them to the surface

might split them

no't really          but if you

Round up          The strokes

sing  'WHAT SIDE ARE YOU ON BOYS'

Trying to Get Home Safe

the table we brought home    had bedbugs    we all agreed to

Spre'd crushed up fossils

Diatoms          aquatic cuties

with sharp bodies

WHO PRODUCE 20% OF THE OXYGEN ON EARTH    [when living] *You used to*

*Get it in your fishnets*          from a boombox on the far side

of the train

Next time on his last in      guys scroll through nudes and semi nudes

turns it so the guy next to him can see:    Green Dress/Long Shirt

Scrolling

Love, no Sunday Morning kinda Lov
This is no ordinary no valentine
This only is a mortal failing love, a cardinal
singingk
singingko
Leaves together making their golden
On the lawn the stairs the slippery stairs So i
how preach to you where sex is political
but only in the Negative, where love i
powerful but only in the smallest moments,
like any magic, and useless against this
to offer such a drought, stuck a concurrent
reflection of a Void, still practicing its sheer
and malice and failing, flexing again-a
snapping
Few, whos never acknowledge directly directly
and malice and failing, flexing again snappin
the Not-worm, the Empty Evil, if nything can

31

all i see is actions

i don't know what to do

with the rest

...e Not-worm, the Empty Evil, if anything can
be empty, if anything can be evil i have seen
both and i have felt both in my first second
and third rapists, felt in the baton on my wrist
the hand on my neck, the whiplash yearning
to breathe...this Not-worm suppressing its
Need to be Close, its Need to be Held, its
Sorrow and Wretched Lonelies, oh my
little solely one, come stat for a wilenplace
of my kidney liver conscience, come rest here
one must say, lest the burden of looking at
each horror of the world, each bored Voidless Horro
of the world set in motion by the Coward

Dusteaters, may you never meet them,
may their corpses already be dissolved

Whose  laundry is this
        -allday train ride
    really an Hour's
You Travel More Than Anyone
James says or Nina says
 *Sayy Whaaaat?* No one says that anymore
        Except as a joke as a joke      most conversations

    becoming serious   &deadly
the labels are working        at the border
        Some can't leave
    Their Sex doesn't match    The Records
        Some can't stay        on crowd-funding sites
            the largest donation totals go to
        military vets & missionaries
To patrol the line / the fence / chain-LINKED / water-sore
        Death & i pull the covers over us for another night

Then Death i have to leav
Could i say why? Why i cannot
        there's no room for me in
wield a womb like a hammer?
        the two bedroom. i fear (the)
Why i cannot speak to my own
        nothing in this moment
mother ever again? My own
        so much as my own sorrow
illness What i don't say i (sw)allow
        i hold Death to my chest
to dress her like my second
        they cry the night through
Death asked me
        home to pillow, pillow
to foster the preteen and teenager,
        to bedsheet to mattress
siblings, i asked for two days to
        mattress to gaptoothed ache
prepare. Did i not call every parent
        I WILL NEVER BE A MOTHER
whose love i trust? Every Death
        This was not Death's gift
in this poem? Did i not read
ough books in small hours on trauma and forgiveness? Did i not
ctice breathing? Did i not beg my memory to release its gnashing
my maws from my joints? Did i not let days darken into night? i

Death beats the history from my face
when i ask Them to
measuring openings
strophe   mouth   water

& food & pepper spray for weeks for months i'm told to prep
for if     for when       they come for us
i've gotten so good at *having a moment*
now
i have days full of them

until the ice cube
won't fit past the lip i bleed
into the water the sound
try to Cover It Up
       this
    Whole BOdy or at least
    like my neck [circle one: bruises or stubble] at work or grief
    for father Death everywhere all the time

today though is harder because?
i left Them and i'm reading Bernadette Mayer
write about Ted Berrigan doing things
while he was alive, but so far only in a dream

    Where i am

Death, in the beginning of The Long Virus, had to feel helpless. And they already feared for years had extracted my need deaths are born of necessity.

ckle need from living breast after longing breast. row busty and hung themself with need, grow muscled d mustached with it. Bulge with its future hurt. Coerce ctors to commit crimes against The American Family giving us life-saving services of Need. Without need, ere would be no joy. And there was no joy in my leaving. ad my own Need to remember. Death too. we began our arching, alone, and weary. What life you find in a toxic eek, fetid with the decomposing corpses, gurgling with tilled after, is all need and miracle.

35

what i want to remember is falling asleep on your chest

Ghostfishing is a beautiful horrendoust name for nets hooks cages traps floating resting on the sea floor and capturing creatures living beings while starve to death inside them or move in the [ ] it the weight of them until they are pried loose from them [ ] the foremost scholars say are [oil off a] Lucky Duck['s] [back]. Artificial Intelligence slaughter machines. let them!! become [ ] and the tools go on killing without creation thinking ever nobody ever i call these nets and cages and traps organs. we might call them body modifications. we might call them vestigial like snail's tails. in the Body of Water they might also be prostheses. here, try to love the water without thinking about the water bottles. i am sick with containers. this one right here of Paper or Plastic? and the one of wince, the one of cloth handmaiden the USA. Made In The USA usually means made by people who are incarcerated, means made by slaves. once over to Death's house at 10:45 pm, and there is a family all holding their hands to the roof of their car. i [ ] i'm the [closest] one who can speak to never wood when i have hands on their weapons. the parents are translating through their elementary school kids. the father is crying. th[e] officers let them Off With A Warning. it's now 11:30 pm in all Death i love. Then as often as i feel i can without being annoying. i tell Death i think the Arm of the Law once made sense? and Death tells me how wrong i am thank God Death says the pigs were always part of the terror state to collect rent or scare people into it and destroy families to remove generational wealth. Overpowered overhyped a boxer's fist violinist's wrist harnessed to capture only and trapping and [ ] loose? inherit now are a military and not gear and the pregnant woman at Walmart gets slammed to the floor for shoplifting and the officers face nothing. not after i recorded and call out the email and video evidence [ ] the reporters at every station Kansas City *Star* office and *Independence Examiner*. nothing and Now? i am locked outside my own home reading a book that doesn't really get it in the same ways i probably don't. in the way it says "i am afraid / i am ridding myself / metonyymic of deth" who i wait or...

so i don't know i don't care

wood beneath [ ] at the end of the hall

he landscape already has changed the screens

mean [ ] hands and flesh [ ] what i has already been.

you have been creating loyally all night what

humiliations [ ] it's [ ] are coming out of their [brew]loops. I hear [carn]ations

will begin to droop and dry there during the parade.

to get home

tissue taking holding. how much remains

i fly fighting despair again another night[?] at least. at least how

much we can care for one another. and the[n?]

like theeeeeee

36

rolling over -- oh good. a cool [ ] f-rom

the sweat pooled, becoming [ ]r in the wild ai

Dandelion tufts forming cities/grids
one two three four
land in my eyeshadow
smudging EACH FULL
EACH EVER
EACH OTHER

no gods today
i can, i can feel it
Soliciting & Gambling
are prohibited

beforehand    aftershocks  little body
wanting to be littler
this domain
always i'mminen't  always   Thanks
Death says  for being the embodiment
of my every fantasy

which i said to?   You too, except
you can't murder me
not that
i really want that, or anything

i know
killing me [like that] is impossible
unattainable
Why(!) it's perfect

Unrequi[r/t]ed lubricant with
A good sense of humor balancing
Trying to Ctrl+Alt+Del
My [pussy/asshole]

no this can't be    BLISTER    my friend

Centered

it • there has to    Body scrape    on the porch

LB. ME  all kinds of

be more for us    wax relics    and the light

handy shortcut keystrokes

But

from white    you invented

Elongated Ours

backwards    [the more

begin to look like Why's

eternity    somehow    I mean?]

begins    on a beanie

here    reading Supyeme    animal anguish of    the door    and the ash

looking up

again ?    into green eyes    closes, Oh    in my mouth.

or brown eyes

spit    or holes    Love, could    The same night

in th ceiling    fan doesn't work

polishing    Yeah the roofer caught the house    this be it?    I earned

ON FIRE    then ran off

along    small-time neurosurgeon students    eternity in    my whiskers

the floured    gaslighting ᵒʳ moonlighting    threes    tallow

floor    burning the midnight    begins With a    barrow

oil vs. grease    cars smoking    smoldering    blush

scrubbing    whimper    pressure cooker ruined the beans Death made

two-handed,    not making up    it swells    abey

for our mistakes

IS THIS    every cat picks on the new cat    and gives    because

new cat hides    Death worries The Muse of History

HOW DOES    is [making red the yellow] on everything    recede nothing    I need

, ONE RECEIVE    every inch of [being/bedding]    with our tongues    is over    lit—

made of nostrils & elbows    fistfulls of cloth    Foucault talking present

THE KISS    more lucid    I am

38

OF A GOD    than bone    Scared,

AND NOT    There was    my Keeper.

i can
no
longer
Wait
for Blessing
and i
no longer
Believe
[ ]
in
revenge
fullflesh
threat THIS
CAN'T BE
IT
DEAR
PITY A
CALL

Instead of Pastilence
i told my cousin to read the MasK of the Red Death
to help him with a song
in one verse the servant works the sewers
and everyone else parties   *promise there's a point to this*   environmental
disaster impending   gratitude   gutterbabe, i think
i may
have
misremembered or misspoke
when thinking of the calendar, all portraits of James' face
12 months of T*his is what i got*
*That's what you git*   new lover, Death, similar  leaves
for New York to dance
while this man across from me
wears socks with bacon & eggs

FOR SAFETY
PROPERTY
ACCEPTANCE
no, there
Is more
, i hide
some way
along warm
thighs under
floods
it melts?
into me
always has
been
a thief
and a
[   ]ward
against

[upperhand—
loss for Love's [ ]
fills its
container
like a [d][]/s]eam
slung fist
may link
each
opens
to let it
[ ]ill
every [d]ought
dread
every
recess
shadow How
polish doubles
the candlelight

Is Trump still president. Another useless question. Let me start over. ii like to go DOW[N/JONES] on
Death What is a mo th?
my hair is the longest it's evrr been. better to hold on to, but Death rips it out
sometimes. there's a rally & march this afternoon. i've become [    ]of crowds.

trying to do anything but nothing. someone says start with telling strangers on the train & coworkers
about municipalities going bankrupt during the 2008 financial crisis & how contractors
told them to balance their books by increasing fines/court fees/etc. for offenders

how's that? Wrong place wrong time Death & i met on a dating app. at the end of our first date Death
put Their Hands
to my face so gently to kiss me, a smile asking for nothing but another to stand

next to. i watched Death get on Their Bike and not very drunk ride away. in Nashville
i was so hopeful i campaigned on behalf of a mayoral candidate when intern becomes internal.

working with a Street Newspaper, sold by people who live outside or who used to,
or who have no permanent residence, and the staff & i went to townhalls, dinners, & who knew

all the other elbowrubbing cowtowing saltlicking leatheroiling assmenagerie
debutante slackjawing backhoeing Ceasar-saladtossing cablecompany NASDAQUIRI

brunchbellying politicking we did to get Megan Barry elected, who decidedly no doubt
spoke during the campaign of fighting for the impoverished & homeless but within no doubt

a month of office had the police force raid the largest tent city confiscate their entire lives
arrest everyone & destroy the showers grills firepits beds cooler systems trails homes lives

put up fencing caution tape. i do not campaign i sleep on a sleeping bag on top
of a yoga mat on top of a purple towel on top of all my sweaters on top

of insulation foam pieces from the air conditioner. for strep throat they gave me penicillin
at the queer center they asked twice if they could touch my neck twice before feeling for my lymph
    nodes

solar ext. f4

drink into did

fill yr mouth

THEnd  swallow    honey

i knew it

all

along

after

all

who knows the real face of choosing to be alive because the alternative is just slightly
more terrifying    last chance

we lock the bikes
to each other & a cement block

Good Fucking Luck

Moving over in w/at

w/to?    Lake?        re : ed

w/t/f
o

n

n n n   n    repainting the barn
yellow

the fingers

yellow the whole sludgedead lushyet world

an iris blooming with pure lavish wrath
op Please. Stop Stop it takes everything to
t count The Horror you are meant to tilt
ur head back There - are to - are so - such
hat are you scared of The clamor sky Yes the
in will tear Off if you do it like that!! not-
time there isn't much the dirt is beginning
taste like porch made ice-cream we shal
art from the commodity the way memories
helplessness are - can e be inventoried
a museum move onto the exchange The
ter gushing parallel from one mouth to an
mobile other we Will attempt to finish with
Given fingernails clacking yes like ice in a
p both of those both are in the room now
realize you ve drinkgd too much? closer
eaning discovering More smaller bruise
you think you are a river that can Low and
w and Low until deep is all gore light thrown
om a spark off three nearly bared teeth

it used to be about the maps, wasn't
``` that rain began

III.

Death fries us some overrripe plantains
    in a greasy cast-iron skillet
        Asks me what to add
    i say chili powder idk?
                So Death says And some sugar

everything, only fitting (as ablue,
address)

    What they're sooo sweet

    Just a little       ... that it should End Us a cumulus

    Death likes The fruit closest to rotten
        The mushy strawberry no one in the house wants
            The things farthest from birth? I wish

thencumberescence carries

that could be a lie
hey ! get easier to tell the older i get        us to
Harder to tell which is which like :

clime and May says call her
September

        how long could it be before i too
                will stop seeing Death everywhere i go

just fir today, i wake up holding y
our breath like a water lily i have
scooped up as a toad. one as the
dust that will come with the rain t
o swallow us up. a black sunspot
in its shoulder, _ umbling ! here i
```

t hops off into the mud and under
growth, a perfect plume of should
i kiss the Gile hair awake at the ro

wish One weren't Two
wish One weren't Two
wish One weren't Two

two to mothmoan threee

three asking hyper-thread-

bare   s[w]ore   notch   belt   -loop   what i know
of strangulation

is how many times

not of your neck? or, should re

turn the lily to its rest, which is

my dad said that's how he would go

white [f]lies     suck out the sap     like u [shouldn't]
snake venom

the

from Death's tomato plants     soap solution   forever laugh
won't wash them away     we harvest them green   well i don't
think hanging

o

from the ceiling would work

f course and you tell me a story. it

a fannannannn&a light     No Weighghghtt! N O W E Y!
to be sure to be safe   louder
than drinking To Death:
Yrself
no Grave
could be called Early

begins with: That was a Good, Stor

y. is it that phrase becomes blurr

where soy & corn play hide n seek every year
were basements     were sheds
where the Kansas Foster Care system
lost track of 74 kids   where hills & hillocks
& cornflowers & chamomile

ied so often? have the moments g

one so soon to the ancestors? sa

y our name again for me, just fir to

where flat         where All's Well
That Ends                     well
                        & the well
                              Is poison

day: clump of Welcome, rain

we have opened every hollow

it is   only     fitting that you,

you       you     Fill it

Not So Many Fears Gather Like Colors

i left & met Death
      on a cold springy night

| | |
|---|---|
| CAUSE | BUILDING |
| FIT | THE |
| AXIS | WILDER |
| ONTO | YOU |
| TITHING | ILL |
| UNDERRAPT | BLISTERIA |
| OF | WHITHER |
| WALKING | UNTIL |
| SCICKLES | UNTIL |
| CIRCLE | OUR |
| EVERREADY | ARRYTHMIA |
| LANCELET | KILLTER |
| IF | THIS |
| ACT | HOLDS |
| HOPE | THEN |
| WELLMIGHTASWELL | |
| FIGURE | TO |
| TRANSVERSE | INSURMOUNT |
| SNAKES | KISSING |
| TELLTALE | NNNNN |
| S I N G L E T S I N G E R | |
| SEWING | MACHINE |
| TURNED | DESK |
| INTERNAL | FLINT-SMOKE |
| OAK | TRUST |
| TURNING | LATHING |
| ASH | DOORS |
| THATS | LoL |
| SO | LUCKY |
| WE | EXIST |

# Not So Many Fears Gather Like Colors

would ∫ honey yearly the muck of / salt — a screech follow — the truth hammered beg(ett)ing as a nautilus Shell? Some terrarium shimmering each wall permits looking and knocking and flummox? fine we shall say Flummox like her light at the everwild rapacious temple building to 12 tasks assigned in repentance would i ask a god for anything Lesst have i not written my final letters and sacrificed them to the candle wick and i Have ∫ accepted suffering now and forever to peril in the arms of one who can take a bLoom and yoke it to the earth like sand and to invite any summerescent fleeting full redeemed refined replenenished to how so? And not so many fears gather barely at the purple pursing echo can you glimpse say one sacrilege quivering counting again your blessings??? mechanical limb made flesh the purpose of a synthetic is to make a stable palette but Ye(ar)s overcoming Ye(ars) of Little Faith toiling to turn the page to guess why the water and air some pure mixture has risen to the front of my mouth and spilling now isn't this the Hell they spoke of isn't this the peace we were so promised let me not take one more yellow breath i am sure i will be forgiven for this extravagance so long as there is a stitch of use and isn't there, love? Why did i say temple building before when now it is only the excavation? When what structure it could become will offer more red than prayer refuge communion? When i have no idea at all what here lateday skyshade founding means When i only now feel this the whole of the ground roiling

handle to fit one finger
                lifted apart where heavy
        &light  separate    culled

Into    Night Terrors^TM
                where Death dreams me into being
& dreams i go to the grocer
-y store to buy watermelon
slices which Death dreams
i call triangles and "almost
too sweet" i'm sticky from
ear to ear and rags of hairs
catch on what Death calls "u-
n cut face grass" just kidding
who cares the day the Sun!

Death dreams Death sits at
an unstable breakfast table
with coffee from across the
  STREEEEEEEET trying to un
Cover the crossword clue
1.      HELP ME! HELP ME!

        [The Module
        "C:\Users\Row\Poemwork\Bookwork\Death Crossword.dll"
        failed to load.

        Make sure the binary is stored at the specified path or
        debug it to check for problems with the binary or
        dependent .DLL files.

        The specified module could not be found.]

**45**

Aug 1.
It is the day i decide i can trust you.

Death dreams Death has more than two than three than four options
Death throws the pen into a bouquet of blue & white & purple flowers
picked from Humboldt Park where Death has me walk not quite
hand-in-hand with a friend who tells me the Angel of Death visited them
& their partner & their friend Hunter standing at the foot of their
beds. Death wondered where Angel went when Death ends Their
Watch prayerless all of us ? in the classical &th Baroque senses Death & i
at least are romantics Blood Messengers fluid bound Th Coal Art of mosquitoes
& viruses guzzle backwash into our DNA strands DO I KISS MY CHILDREN
WITH THAT MOUTH like an insect that is one of our greatest pollinators
tho Sometimes takes a lil blood for their eggs and everyone goes BERSERK
GANGBUSTERS A(W)OL Online Death dreams Death multiplies with my sperm
& it is clearly the Trans Messiah says Death's friend since Death & i are both
sterile Death scrolls thru thendless Feed never full never empty idle th oughts
& ends not quite Their suggested Friends & Followers quoting & quipping
as when Death looks in the mirror in Their dream & the mirror wakes up
Death Two-Faces everything bringing all the products to the fore & putting
Names & Logos outward so the customers have the impression that WE ARE
REPLETE no wait that's what i do i'm always projecting like the movies on our
first date WE ARE FULL-Y Death's nipples are always on display but back
Death dreams me at the grocery store selecting pre-made salsas & dips &
flour tortillas eating Them from afar

on the bus my tuck
comes, Death dreams,
undone the bulge im
-possible to fix within
& without alerting the
seated passenger next
to it but i am filling the
correct AMT MACHINE
of space either/orchi[d]-
ectomy u can't have it
a lb. of feathers or a lb.

In the dark of a humblit fix... blade on
my shoulder... rhymes with dew one everyday.
Because my pants pove... smear other underneath
the taut plastic... sleeping... straws... chest
the sweat pools... pixel... draw with straw. For
straw, scatters... Bones... ... br...
from my nose... wound to take a womb of hair in
your hand and pull... this time hear the bones com
together.
i don't understand... social... style. i was a coup
blocks with M... ... i...
her Daddy carry a large table out to the van and
Daddy is shouting... i got it. Don't drop this A–
this is really expensive!" What am i getting myself
into--but... fun. Too bad C–'s already at her
Daddy's place... named P– who wants to do
everything... but is too close to see and keeps
packing the very large boxes a third full. M says hi
briefly to... and we chat in a small, disparate way,
and i feel weird about mixing worlds--even though
this is the only one and it is changing so much so
rapidly at the coincidence of greedy, pathetic hand
clapping off-beat to the war drums. Nonetheless
maybe more so, the reluctance

of castor oil lingering in
    my side which is heav-
    ier  ? ANYWEIGH [us l i c e it]    Death dreams

        Death sees Dogs necking
Or
        Dogs eating each other's necks
Or
        Dogs licking their wounds
            But Dogs is Death's best friend & Dogs
is coming over for brunch
        Dogs is trying to quit adderall
Or
        Slow Down

            obsolete starlight pulsing
                into the bedroom where Death dreams
after the grocery store open the door it creaks it sticks it bulges with my knee
        I ENTER    EXEUNT
        I ENTER EXEUNT

        I ENTEREXEUNT I ENTER EXEUNT I ENTER
        EXEUNT.EXE I ENTER TO THE SOUND

        Of Death pulling a blanket over Their lowerhalf
        Death dreams  "This is how I get murdered
        This is it." Death & i laugh. Death dreams we laugh

Death wakes up
                          Half-light discarding itself
Nnnnnnn n nnn nn       single serve
    O o ooooo ooooo    window-pane
                        dissolves into lactose-
                        free cheddar & coconut oil (Virgin)
Death                    melts
    around my fingertips

    Death puts a finger on my nose says
    BOoOP! i say YR A DREAM

    we make coffee grinding free samples from my work
        gets caught in the filter   in Death's empty joints we read
more news                      trying to stay
    of the administration's         human    alive
        fascist border policy         longer
                      or rub each other's shoulders
                      in a kitchen where no one notices
    us        but the cats   & they meow
                they hunger
                their shit needs picking up
    the chickens        cluck cluck cluck the
                Sunflowers Miracle
           GROW ALL MORNING
        THEY grown't enow

        to stop being eaten

    when it didn't snow today      [How could it]

the day b4 me & the first-Death-i-met's 9 year anniversary
          this new deep cavern love i have for Death reminding me
     when i first tripped down Their Mine [shaft] & stopped looking for places to land
              a light or a ladder or a rope or a handhold or telling & how much deeper
          i might fall into Death How
     taking a walk

to see what?

...s was when I had their friend tell that gossip ...ece over the phone about these fancy boots she had ...t from her sugar daddy and then sold and replaced ...th knock-offs that they wore more. A real threat of ...olence. God it was so ... private ...t it was publicly ...ly the frantic retelling and ...e fact that the storyteller was alive, I guess that was ...e central point. made it hilarious. I was so nervous ...y I wonder because I was sitting next to my trans- ...d? And the body became the screen for a while, ...cked with the degradation from the eggshells ...aring into the physical film during development. ...uch a cool window. I touch the cold hand to my ...eek. Already i am lost, then back in the room. You ...n see so many specific emotions when you divide ...ace, even in a gasp or a bawl, though a smile is so ...l it might be a good start for beginners. Let me ...plain: look at a photo of someone you love. Place ...ur hand over half of their visage. Now the other ...lf. Now horizontal, or vertical. Now, just one eye. ...w, just the corner of their mouth. Now, their cheek ... you see? Some emotions don't reside in the face, ...pending on the person. Don't be frustrated if you ...n't see something you are certain must be there ...ght away. For instance, when i look at this photo of ...aughing with unutterable joy on their porch couch ...o not see the rage. Maybe because they are turned

**BLUE LIVES MATTER stickers on two BigBoy**
Vroom Vroom trucks parked in my neighborhood reading
two articles—one about a successful rally hmm wonder And
one about what a girl needs and how to be safe when i walk
home @night so i'm less scared & so i don't break out into
a run or tears or sing loudly whistling or whatever playing
back from work or taking the train the-ann walking but morning
they say is worse they say "a little paranoia is really good
for every woman" & i am paranoid born & raised *but not as*
*a woman* so i say the spells to make people go away
i'm just using a different cauldron & it requires different sounds

i never learned So i invent a few "oh god yr so cute i wish
my boyfriend wasn't waiting on me i wish my husband didn't
keep me on a leash i wish I had autonomy" open wide AHHH
TON O MEEEEEE OH MY OH MEEEE on the train the man asks
me what i'm reading then tells me I Love Red-Headed Women
No Joke i tell him & he cuts me off & says That's Why We Could
n't Be Together You Were Always Talking That Shit then says Lem

Me Ask You: Are You All Female? / i sayyyyyyyy *Not According To*
*The Government.* / So You're Not. So, So You're Not. Hm. So You're
You're Not. Not. Could've Fooled Me. Fuuck. Fuuuuuuuuck. Fuck.
Could Have Fooled Me Fuck Fuck. Fuuuuuuuck. [it's my
Stop.[ [pls. stop] he says it low & soft to himself. COULDHA FOOLED ME. FUCK. FUCK. he says
to the rest of the empty car stays me & him & now
waiting at the door. the door takes a long time to open at the platform.

Death is in the hospital. i haven't spoken to Death in years. I say, Mom. Are you going to be ok? She says the distance between us the plants the wind chimes between doorways ring sometimes and that is how she knows i'm thinking of her. She says I Didn't Realize a lot. She talks about Death and how much she loved him. How high the suicide rate of long-term interferon patients is. i say i think capitalism killed Death. i don't say I Don't Blame You. She says how a filter is changed in the water treatment facility; how fast she had to type for the Sprint relay job. We go on. Death buries a hatchet in the door to my sibling's room. She mentions this i don't know why any of this is here.

...to the openings, openings are everything, he said. It will spill out. So she taught me this method of reading, of being read. i wonder if it began before i remember? To dissect and know that anyone might at any moment be vivisecting. If you practice it, you might find yourself always at it. With the masks the way they are i suppose i should have ought to... for with... at all of your... into my... to suck... i... genuine... anything... that y tongue resembles. When i leave M and the rest of NYC i also leave a favorite shirt behind on accident. shirt he left behind in Chicago. i wore it one too many times as a compost bucket washer and the bleach gave it some strange discoloration on the left side of the belly. It is the part of me that aches when s send a photo of their perfect, plundering ass next his girlfriend's. i do not know how to section an ss and read it. A says there's a palmistry for reading sses, when she's nauseous from the new meds e're taking. And i wonder if this is when i should ll her that i love her for the first time. i've been king myself that all yesterday and all today. At the rd sanctuary near the lake shore, the chickadees ling the nearly bare trees with so many songs and unds. How they approached us. But that is a long

51.

Wu Tsang's film, this dissection happens, is happening with Beverly Glenn-Copeland's hands, face. Necessarily. Tenfold. Stretched larger than a person. Beyond facial expression, into body language. As his stratospheric features before a silver stand microphone rinses the room in a blooming of... the small currents in the spiraling space reshape the curtain and its ripples--if only slightly as the camera pans or doesn't. Who are you to say what you have seen? Who are you to say frolicking and not vile? Do you see it? I ask someone else, someone i've just met—one of T and A's friends--if she sees the curtain moving. No... everasten... have the thin earth. Or is it only the film projected, and its own movement suggesting a doubling. She says... and thinks the curtain is not in fact rippling. It's just the film, panning. When i meet someone, i try not to look at their face very much. It feels intrusive. It feels like a lot to engage with when someone is saying a word you could not have expected and takes perhaps minutes to realize that was their name and what was it? They were moving their hand a little, maybe i should have shook it. When i first met you, you were wearing a mask and sitting on your porch. It was cold and we talked for an hour. Me on the sidewalk, talking up. You, a mountain. To see one from far away the obvious beauty. And all the rewards of looking closely. The life it holds the clear water it...

i did away _ \ wit th
i did toward / with h _____ (name for a group of taxidermists)

should we follow?   Quick! said The Bird   my hand
an  a shadown  crow w/ONE wing in
a mosquito puddle   in the park  Death dreamt of

You are not here!   You are N O NNNOO  T HE AR
To verify
AROSE !  AROSES AROSES AROSES AROSE

the fire & the rose are One          they start

OUT  the same in lungs   but this park trashcan fire needs so
Much More breath i'm tryin i'm tryin i'm tryin
To figure       who owns my debt

not sure if committing credit card fraud  TODO What
nnnn  ooN oONNN N ?   feel like i'm doing something like?
Listening to Rape Revenge's *Paper Cage*

wanting memory   to unbutton
its shirt, starting with
its cuffs, one-handed, then from neck down

hang its shirt on the back of a chair  & lie down   in the tub shower

curtain drawn   hot   so hot the water from the head
let Memory swallow   as it slides

open the box-cutter
let it drag the blade
plowing   the throat  Cold

but not frozen     for the spring  beds  she says
  godless freshness    Death&i watch Lady Lee&hubby
  plow  her first field     farrow-stepping kids in puffy coats

  &we think abOut    having our own, in a fantasy where we
  Love ourselves enough to make more of us in a fantasy the Were-We
  Live in a world That wasn't! slo-LY CH o King on our exhaust

Getting ready to cough   me&Death
  up like  i am now       trying to quit
  these cigarettes        For Good!   for better or
of course of course ofc no stable us    Death purs [sic? em!]
  a tongue & a finger into me until i say No words

  perfect devastation    until the pillow on my face
makes me shiver & the blanket & taking the blanket off
until Death kisses my nose which makes me cum again 3xcept

  for a moment to forget Everything We Dreamed & EVERYTHING I JUST SAID EXCEPT

  I Love You     forget that too forget the beginning forget the word

To practice   *happy* without     throwing it
  into the storm drain  like this   my split-heel sneaker
  quiet shoe-strings oil drugged rain days not
  to drink or pass by   one day &
  soon  & soon enough
  to be summer

53

## IV. when i come home from arranging items according to their expiration dates

Death is sleeping in a stuffy hot room
Death worked all day too
No one on the Red Line noticed
Death was off the clock

i try to off the clock too
That's Not My Department
Slips out of my mouth
Or out of my manager

Learning to serve
She is her Master's Maid
&serves for wages the more
i think i have the more

i have to lose the trick is
Give it Up in a heat index of 110
i like a new burn for how
Smooth my skin feels

When I talked to Them They said
Do You Want Some Pepper
Spray for the late nights
&i shouldn't have said i

Was going to test it
On myself Just To See
Seemed to upset Them
i think you should know

...down the box of farm produce at the delivery
...dress like from a school's dissection lab i come
...on the entrails aren't legible they'rve barely here

How it feels when you Treat Someone
i want to know exactly how much pain
Is Too Much & if damage   Oh well

...cada let us throw the cinder blocks from the stairs
...e cold clings like grime under faucet handle shook
...d shook the tile from the wall she began shoving

i don't think it's permanent

...e glass in it only possible hole the ground was soft
...e fire low the sliding mirros resemble a guillotine
...uld do just fine trembling the wooden panels by
...hat is it other than a shriek a blue shriek we brush
...r hair and they compliment the fresh seaweed
...lored paint i miss you who cares i miss you and
...is won't make the night go by any quicker slower if
...ything i dig my toes into the carpet the possibility
...ce a hand is within a body is so grave a triumph and
...w discipline breaks she began shoving the glass in
...s only possible hole the ground was not soft enough
...e had to bring a shovel forward then a pickaxe dull
...ll dither dancing what is this trembling meant

Teleconsumption N O R I G I N

...ainst the wooden panels by what is it other than a
...riek yes this one too a blue shriek we brush her hai
...d they compliment the fresh seaweed-colored pain
...iss you i care i miss you and this won't make the
...ght go by any quicker slower if possible if anything
...g the carpet with my toes the possibility wants once
...hand is within a body is so grave a triumph and now
...scipline breaks she began shoving the glass

its only possible hole the ground was soft and fire low
the sliding mirrors resemble a guillotine would do just
fine trembling the wooden panels by what is it other
than a shriek a blue shriek we brush her hair and they
compliment the fresh seaweed colored paint i miss you
who cares i miss you and this won't make the night go by
any quicker slower if anything i dig my toes into carpet

**1000 SQ FT OF PROVERBIAL ALIMONY COFFEE BREATH**

the possibility once a hand is within a body is so grave a
triumph and now discipline breaks she began shoving

**ALLLLLBELLYACHTE SIR CH**
the grass got a greener prenup

call in call today
call off call nnnnnnn   ooooooooo   wwwwwwwww

the glass in its only possible hole the ground was soft
and fire low the sliding mirrors resemble a guillotine

at work they pay me to hide my body

bling the wooden panels by what
is it other than a shriek a blue shriek we brush her hair
and they compliment the fresh seaweed colored paint i

**THIS THUS THE APRON HAT SHOECOVER GLOVES ASPMASK CATECHISM CLASSES**

miss you who cares i miss you and this won't make the

We only sell food without preservatives

night go by any quicker slower if anything i dig my toes

Death is banned from my store

into carpet the possibility once a hand is within a body
is so grave a triumph and now discipline breaks like
cheap necklace stripped she began shoving the glass in
its only possible hole the ground was soft and fire low

**F O R T H E F T**

the sliding mirrors resemble a guillotine would do just
fine trembling the wooden panels by what is it other
than a shriek a blue shriek we brush her hair and they
compliment the fresh seaweed colored paint i miss you
who cares i miss you and this won't make if anything i
dig my toes into carpet the possibility once a hand is
within a body discipline breaks

if no danger then no laughter? then no passing of. or more of. try to remember
ecstasy. put a bra on. take one off. the change in pressure is what hurts. right ear
still won't work. after the flight. hold the phone to it. somehow hear the words.
who is screaming. can't tell. yellowbrownpurpleblack bruises play adam's apple.
spell good morning. re:currence. *that thogh he hadde me bet on every bon, / he
koude wynne agayn my love anon. onanon.* the question of repression & if that
is. drone low swells resonant frequency: 5 Hertz. become earthquake machine.
tectonic rift. trauma events &/c/or dissociative. empty memory. f_ll in the gaps.
fingers to a mouth. sovereign boy. *this would require understanding transness
as a matter not of who one is, but of what one wants. the primary function
of gender identity as a political concept—and, increasingly, a legal one—is to
bracket, if not to totally deny, the role of desire in the thing we call gender.*
dear oscillator, the body asks. so intense: to stretch: out: one must forget. or so
deep. the body could not communicate. construct a narrative. this. then. that.
happened to. the body but not the i. closed off. shut

57

down. detour. exit. Mourning [home] is so erotic. oh loss. undecided wound. *This is fucking nonsense.* way out of the way. no noise no light no touch no sensation from the body recognizable. at all. call it hallucinating. *Call this something else. Last night it had a name, / a name wedged between an organ's teeth.* call it delirium. no(?) true reference. the closest: a quarter of shrooms. all shake. & two tabs of acid. DMT at the peak. but that's a different kind of eternity not close to one we're availing. even that / a body remembers but not the climax lasting longer than ___ itself. look at the time! hours of: a mouth swallows a body gulping tongue. *the way she kisses you, her lies wide open.* lungs try. too tight. fingernails into a nipple. Death straddled legs can't kick. remember saying "oh fuck holy shit oh no no no yes please please hurt me dig into me choke me thank—how how how how how" but it sounds like "ow." *What thyng is it that wommen moost desiren.* ask but the ringing. *I trowe I loved hym best for that he / was of his love daungerous to me.* but the feeling gone. not hard to say. impossible. never was quite. no memory but the skin. bad reception. down here. first impressions. "yr too much." put a bandana around a neck. pull. all day the body recalls. here it comes. reef. square. knots made of muscle. shoulders ache. there there. to speech their own. say possession. say domicile. within. a tight shirt on. press digit to. semblance. close. enough. virtual desire. icon or index. a finger is hexkey. a whole hand is catch. dry mouth. not in but around. if no round. then a.

core    call inter
      rupt  ur  e  ffigy
             v   eal
Death drips    i   roning
  A comforter    s  ola  r
    Onto me      c  ###
    The cover becomes  [e s c]hewing
        Slick       r o x
   In the shower     tall a rooo hoo
     Greet         t int
  A thorax    recluse     E Roses
   ^(Cephalo-)       do   it
       Death picks    me
    Apart

      One     by     One

sugar maple tree should be nearly forty years old before you can tap it safely. Before the tree is roughly ?" in diameter, the risk of systemic microbial infection the tree becomes very large and probable. It is the maple tree leaves that produce antimicrobial properties. In the same... they prevent a spread, though the organisms... not kill the microbes themselves. As those antimicrobial compounds flow from the leaves through the capillaries to the roots, they prevent... greater cost. In a smaller tree, this system is less developed, and the depth of the tap is much more dangerous for its relative size. Certainly, a smaller sugar maple will produce delicious sap nevertheless. Is a matter of sustainability. Tapping sooner than you should will also stunt the growth, and may mean the maple will never reach its potential height or sap production. Will take a much longer time. The sap itself, while not usually toxic to someone adding it their granola, can be contaminated to an unusable degree. To slow the spread of the microbes, many sugar bush farmers have used disinfectants, formaldehyde tablets, and various metal alloys to prevent microbial infections and molds in higher risk trees. These contaminants could reach—but they were saying what a terrible week it has been for bad relationships. And good ones that needed to change.

i was never one     body & though     it might make
things look easier          i don't          know-how
reduced to          *Get it, girl!*          it might make
what with?          the bacteria          my gut the air
in my chest          (i know)          i could not be
in one place          at one time:          the water
i once called *Mine*     the 75%-78% of My     Body That Was
          & the straw     *That broke bitch*
calamity Whose          took it out of me? *distance*
     *coming closer*          i laughed & shouted & cheered
          one or two tears          *Have you failed to make yourself*
     to spread myself          i did not sob thankfully
i've never tested               my mascara in public     name
pockets by how many     fingers they     hold     *Is Nothing Sacred?*
sounds they make          play Dig          -ing is

                    to be active          more          over
          plot me on a graph     i am here! and          here
               x     &     y          not          u & i
     is *Time Elapsed*     &     is *Hope* (mL)     *here*          *Let's Play*
if we glide o (l  a  b  i (&)  a) s  k  e  w     even here     *Left for Dead*
     this               &     ER          OS          I O N     at DELPHI
     Is               &          marathon     failure     L Y C H
     WhAT          &          too late     too late     come back
     i               &     u     n     Der Die Das     How many times  can
     MEAN          &          /or     Mask. Fem. Neu.     (meaning *new*)
                    &c
                    &c
                    &c

**60**

V.

Death & i walk to the beach where

AS IF I HAVEN'T LIVED MY ENTIRE GLUED
GLUTTED SLAUGHTERREADY LIFE ON THE
FULCRUM UPON WHICH EVIL SWIVELS

had begun to lash out. i had stepped on a
broken floorboard with my bad ankle. i started
saying i needed to rehome the kitty that walked
in my back door on boxing day. i put malicious
things in my mouth and laughed.

was years before i realized i had never seen
a teeter-totter up close. presently i stared
straight into the crooked wet base of one. my
great-grandmother was getting older and her
large family came to celebrate. she called me a
beautiful girl and so did the woman at the diner
on the way home. my family believed it was a
mistake, bad eyesight, poor judgment. i was 12,
and i climbed on the see-saw. my hair floated
in the wind as the machine fell in on itself. the
mud—

# IF WHAT I KNOW OF D[ ]EAD IS ONLY [ ] ERROR

the kitty keeps attacking the other cat. i said would flick his balls enough that i would neut him myself and then i laughed because i mean it as some kind of dark joke, a masquerade of when i was little and had seen my mother do this to a child. of my father picking up a cat and throwing it against a wall or kicking the dog for eating its own shit because it had been beaten before for shitting somewhere it wasn supposed to. when the dog Katie needed to go the emergency vet because she was constipat the doorbell rang and the Dominoes pizza guy said i love Dalmatians. the next day he bough her for 40 dollars. Is there how i began to kno relief.

wheee s[w]ore
up & down
Once More
once more

## IF EVERY COMFORT I HAVE KNOWN IS THE DIRECT RESULT OF SUFFERING AND EXPLOITATION

had begun to tease her with a gruesome object that made a terrible snap when you hit someone with it. bu[t i] never hit her and soon her mouth was drool and her [gu]m was on the floor and i couldn't believe our pleasure [w]as so easy or so powerful. though i had known it s[o] [si]mply before with them, week after week. the weeks [fo]lded in on themselves and i said I will only love you [fo]r the rest of my life, but this was a joke not because [of] monagamy but because time was spilling from her [at] such a rate i would never arrive beyond the present [i] was to live for an eternity in her drool-stuffed [co]mforter muffled gibberish. elsewhere the time had [sl]owed in relation, and soon we were both before and [af]ter the rest of existence. so i said the unforgiveable [un]truth again.

earthwarm
rainwater
skipping stones
skipping home

Into The Teyed

tilled till'd opal
basil sweet weeds all is
chicken feed

even in those many moments that became one i thoug
of him, when i first understood what pleasure wa
wrapped around his fingers, living in His ecsta
sometimes when he and i talk, it is as if he has forgott
what we discovered together. as if the bodily euphor
went away. HOW IS IT SO HARD TO RECALL PLEASUI
WHEN TERROR RINGS FALSE LIKE FREEDOM FRO
THE LIBERTY BELL, FABRICATED, COMMODIFIE
CLOTTED AND FLOWING MOTTLED, DULL ECHO (
ITS GESTURE, THE SOUND OF A DOG DROPPING
DRY BONE—NOW A DROOLWET BONE—ONTO FL.
CARDBOARD, INSISTENT AND ACCOMPANIED 1
as if i have forgotten. despite writing it all down. a;
blabbering blubbering to so many people i trusted wh
joy i was learning.
two hours passed and passed again we were pull
back into when we are now. when i hope you are n
pillowbound beneath her orgasms. we worm into t
spaces we created in each other, pulled the dirt over o
steaming bodies, and fell asleep as the sky darkene
when they awoke she had that devil at dawn look. a
she was the _east. and so she turned. over like a garde
all flesh is harvest. the last leaves. already turning a-

IF TERROR IS AN AMBIENT EN
UNCERTAINTY A MOMENT BETWEEN OCC
RECOGNITION
TERROR IS AN AMBIENT ENCOMPASSING
NCERTAINTY A MOMENT BETWEEN OCCURENCE AND
ECOGNITION
AS IF TERROR IS A MEASURE OF RISK

CLOSELINE

S IF TERROR IS A MEASURE OF RISK
AS IF TERROR IS THE PALPABLE RISK ITS

S IF TERROR IS THE PALPABLE RISK ITSELF

if you have any physical money on you at this mome[nt]
you can skip ahead or go back! to page [numb]
of your coworkers who have never had to go in
work sic[k] at risk of 'Pointing Out' or getting fir[e]

**AS A AS Y**
Window  wHy_per   glass Cut_er

multiplied by the hours you have come to terms wi[th]
the coward's despair of the yet implacable fact y[ou]
were not strong enough to overcome the suici[de]
ideation, this time. add this to the number of tim[es]
you have truly forgiven your mother]. if you do[n't]
have any money on you, think of something re[]
about forgiveness. tell someone about this. RIG[HT]
NOW GO NO FURTHER UNTIL YOU HAVE DONE S[]
who is the most forgiving person you have know[n]
Do you think you would like to live like that? i ha[ve]
stopped taking public transit because of the consta[nt]
harrassment i attract. today i don't bike the 9 mi[les]
to the queer clinic because i am tired. WHY A[M]
CURSED TO TELL THIS SAME STORY? four mo[re]
years later almost the exact sentence. i place stic[k]
bandages on the sores i think are pox then dress[]
long sleeves tights and a loose denim skirt. sweati[ng]
through i keep my mask on just in case. it is strange[]
think i don't know what forgiveness could look l[ike]
on someone's face. it is strange to think i don't kn[ow]
what the hardest bout of forgiveness my best frie[nd]
has had to battle. it is 84 degrees and i drink up t[]

In the street
       Baby cries
The MUSE OF HISTORY squints

up the sunlight. i am gay and caught the new disease because the [lowercase D] death cult has failed to worship Death properly. the government and its bored violence. the inattentive handlers with their long leashes and ruthless, inconsistent corrective beatings. the attentive handlers and their constant affections. i get on the train and a man touches me within minutes, asks me about my hair. i tell him i have the new virus and am going to get medicine. he leaves me alone to a book. at a stop downtown the train whirrs to a halt. the conductor says 'They shut off the power.' Who's they? i ask the train. the person across from me points at their mask and winks. The police arrest someone and the station gets shut down. so i start walking. my keys jangling with hurry makes a lot of people look over their shoulders. i am gaining on them. at the queer clinic the guy who says i'm too late for my monkeypox screening also says The trains have been getting dangerous. People are desperate, he says. Quickly, he looks around the clinic.

# AT THE END OF FORGETTING BEGINS THE SEARCH

we attach candles to their brass holders and carry them. im in a big, big shirt. when she calls me her daughter she says *you will always be my son and you look so much like your dad it hurts.* i light her her cigarette with my candle flame. the fire is the only sacred thing and the fire takes everything from us. the power is not out we are fearful of the light entering the outside the curtains closed over blinds underneath loose fabric from the fabric store where i wait in the basket of pillows how long does this take. take two candles around the house we start on the ungrouted cold tile of the back room. to place a foot tippytoes and touch a clump of shorn hair. to know the difference between dread and horror. to the dark is imminent and/or ambient, to lick the folds with a cut fingertip the folded cloth and touch a broken piano key, its soft thud like a cardinal landing on a snowy branch. if you listen the light grows and her breath why does it sound like rain is this shivering.

volume of: folded hands
dropping to yr knees
wat    er
that mouth
dew
wind    resistance

6

the colder basement cement steps painted a
rest green why it's too late in the flickering in
e one aim to question motive there is a danger
e are seeking my mother tells me her mother
ade her do this and how she hated it sitting
th a shotgun on their laps waiting for daylight
grampa Don to come time we open a door
the garage the basement covered in mildew
rpet path Each door begins the terror
ain i am and then scared and do you believe
is not for an impossible intruder but for the
nd grabbing my shoulder it is the cold or the
t of the carpet to the cement floor it is the
pport beam touch i think we descend further
d there is no safety who is asking for it the
een door creaking window checks every window
pecially the tiny ones by the fireplace that not
en a small fantasy could slither through in
e darkest form of the house the furthest from
e natural exits i am going to Forget the worst
it to wait for a friend to tell me What I Have
st the Loss becomes equilibrium and the fear
otidian to approach an approaching i vow to
no one i love to live in fear of

P   T  [O?]  S   D          a s ur e
                              me

                              du_ty
[ not a chance]        old bag              wl_th by
                       I breathe in          length by
                                             Hiiiiiiiii [t]
            Death holds the hen
[ in hell                warm  X  tight
lacewing                 says He's so soft!
Butterflies
bumblebees
rubbing their              beachblack night
wings wiiiiii[]            strip
their back                 Death stands thigh-high
legs can't                 ice-cold
move past                  Lake Mosquito
the window
realbits? Rabbits
maybe sure
standstill
shift their
handsand wait
for children
to snap their        no    nnnnooo nooo noooo nnn nnnn nn
necks Hell                thing        worth
is filled wi th          stealing
sound of        i have too much    sticky-notes!     petroleum!
rejoicing                peanut butter!

            give it!    nnnnnnnnn ooooooooo   you !
            to someone
                        Who Needs It?!!!!!

69

## VI.

somewhere along the way i bega
covering myself in INSECTICIDE
MITICIDE · ANTIFUNGAL before goi
to sleep. before going to sleep she wri
les the unforgivable calculations fo
the expanding universe onto my cur
All she needs, she says to the only roo
of light in the apartment, is the shado
and the measure of its angle. An
exactly the same second minute an
hour, a thousand and twenty ston
throws away, the woman she loves
also trembling in some sort of feedbac
loop, like the slow dial of a tuning p
bringing a note together with. the rat
of the time between echoes ? pulse:
can be extrapolated into the heavens

a tell-tale telemachina
Home(weary)war_

GIMME THAT D

GIMME THAT E

GIMME THAT A

GIMME THAT T

GIMME THAT ACHE [ay-chuh]

Death&i walk to the center of a
hedgemaze    9yrs ago
we kiss the branches
at the entrance &everwhere else

we return to the Sorceress
She tells us there's
a mouse named Mick in the trap —this is true –
we make him [asphyxiate/headless/a bowl of soup/a lifelong friend]
so we can feed him

To The Hens,                    to Make Much of Time
Gather y'all's wildflowers while y'all may
Soon the coop will close y'all in for the night
Rather than suffer the slings of day
Croon y'all's sockless toes the dirt of composted
Light y'all's candles at every end & every beginning
For those who come after you & those who?
Came before & same the blighted scowl, i
Cuddle a dog who cuddles Death—tomorrow the fog

i tell Death a story to help them sleep

    a bridge and two people walk
    a long it. the bridge is wood.
    some metal bands. the bridge
    cracks. beneath the bridge
    the ground. far enough. too
    far to see the rocks and say
    tfeir names as if you saw them
    anywhere that wasn't
    a patio furniture catalog.
    home repair masonry.
    on th bank these words

```
   p  run      I n g
  ill      est
 home    s     ic
  win h o  w?  ell
 a   p o s t r o p h e y
     in      't
     d    o  wl
     a t     h
pppp ppppppppppppppppppppppppppppppp
```

    between THE MUSE OF HISTORY and Mugwort and me
    y er gues s is as good as mine as to(mb!)
    who is the stuffed animal who is the purring kitty who is Death's plaything and

    who makes Death smile in Their sleep
      pawprints on the comforter
    i dream
     we are a family
    the many Deaths&i

dream
           we are blood
           i dream
               the table
           [d]ream
               the tyrant
           -me looks Death in Their
               wide-lens gorg-[on/ing/ous]

               eyesocketseye

             am matchbook empty st-
             ripped of[f] spark i am
           stolen pocketed snuffed
         like those films
         when i first  arrived
        digitally
     looking for Death
teaching myself         to cry
teaching myself    to look  to listen
                 |        |
           A screwdriver    a bloodscream
           A stomach       a trachea full

         in low fidelity    the laughter
         c[r]ackles

             learning what
             what the fuck should anyone know
         i don't remember
         seeing a light go out
         only still

             as the moon @dawn

---

hat was that? a fragment becomes figment
nd i turn on all the lights in my ground-
oor apartment. deadbolt the doors and
eck the windows, i put a heavy chain
ong my mattress. the sounds become
ien in semi-stereo. i hear the whisper of
voice or a footfall. keys? creaking i hear
nest of hatchlings and they are being
d. a gun safety clicking. a knife sliding
om its woodblock. this is how i practice
rgiveness i turn on the last light in my
ouse and say, I Am Scared. I Am Trying to
ake Sense of An Uncertain Evil. i close my
es and try to sleep.

BECAUSE I BECAME AN AGENT OF EVIL
because every name i have accepted has come fro
Death. when Death, my ex-wife, gave me my nam
it was a mineral. it meant Crumb. or it meant
Glitter. Death had said, I found the perfect litt
name for you. And when i split they would s
WHAT PERFECT [BASAL] CLEAVAGE. i had so ma
uses. i could be lubricant for the molding of rubbe
because of my platy morphology i could, if i g
ground up be a pigment extender for paints. th
sounded cool. i wondered what kind of paints an
pigment. i thought about the fig and the firmamen
how pigs are so pink or covered in dusky hair. ho
nothing up there feels steady at all. but i decide
to became glass the oven would get very hot bu
wouldn't. i was them that i would see through to t
roasting root vegetables. Death asked where i wa
already i had begun using another name. becau
Death had shown me a flower that had all kin
of uses. t all healing. which
thought was found by some was Death who w
mending of tearing up the fi
layers of the upstairs bathroom. Dea
was walking around the dan
festival making sounds like a phone. or vying f
position in front of the self-facing camera extend
apparatus. i was charming Death's parents becau
i hadn't told them i was an Agent of Evil.

[n]E[i]ther  days
[n]O[r] nights!

i thought i might   remain calm
through violence     making action possible?

Instead of remaining still &stiff
choking
[i say]
i read online is the only kink
[it is?]
impossible to make safe
[o i c]
sterile        sharpbucket i
ask Death to come while they
throttle me      The nightmares
started long before

long before i dreamt
Death&i sleep under a micetree
nails scratching the hardwood branches
teeth on carpet is chitterchatter
the soft worry that   no raccoon would ever whisper

yr name as they fell asleep, not like that
not like This: Mouth a crescent moon entering
each other's dreams to play in a [oil]field
Daisies Sunflowers Sackrin Sycamore Spotted
Toadolescents Begonias Conical Sections of A
Mountain't That Something HYPERBOLAS yes im
Agine the other other half  Honeycomb Rotted Rusted
Hatchbacks   Empty of Nothing But
Gasoline Guppies licking our faces sleeping
Capone the Pup kicks us awake ancient lightning

Threw the [dark/window] closing shut
The sound of styrofoam rubb[er/ing/le]
The sound of the last Devil grating his palms on each other
The sound of his expectation, the sound of his cold
Death closes the door
the blinds
turns out
The light

[the body]

was Front        medicine cabinet me
too        of
broad        spectrum
antibiotics

bcos i could not
stahph for Death

They stomped my heels for me
My whistle morning singing self
And mortgage lender fees

i washed my hands—no blood, no skin—
Twenty-eight times today
i came home to sweet Death's Throne
To dismantle every grain

They did They don't Death kissed my throat
i toe-danced belly-up
tTh sunless evening bumblebee
Had flown inside Their touch

ath believed i was a flight risk and took my new name proof. Dear earth tried to prune me. Before all that eath was this: Death had a cousin-twin, whom loved like summer. their parents mistook each other r each other. if i... way's away. Death and this twin ew older and Death impregnated my mother. The twin now nothing only that i was given the twin's name d that the twin and his motorcycle slid under a semi uck. in my room, my mother hung a picture of a saint th my name slaying the devil. in a poll, 68% of Americans id they believe angels and devils walk among us and fluence the world. i usually ride my bicycle, but if i have take the bus people tend to speak to me unprompted mething i have to get out ahead of. i wonder. they de nd to treat me like a threat or something to be possessed cause i am an Agent of Evil i say, O thank you! and O rry oh ... my friend's forehead and say it is Ward. It extends to everyone they love. for this is my wer. from ... understand the Devil used to work r one of ... didn't like it and my namesake s sent as Divine Muscle. A Tough. Heaven's Thug. well at's just fine, there are many Heavens to serve, and they irl around like a tooth in a mouth. and there are just as any serpentine Devils to hold the necks of with my heel it whisper tongues gagging the air. eyes protruding.

A jar of Honey poured oer mine eyes
   Crystalhard as They
   That Death that lush Their Glut that hush
   A metal lathe a cave[ u]rN O Us

dribble tooth i fell asleep on Their arms
but wake now alONe aloe nnnn aloan
might take the ice cream scoop
to these lousy eyes

or wishing else for a tree branch
to split me   when i fall
from the office where i used to work
dangling from my noosey intestines coal
?
   but once a month or so often
  soupy little thing this wanted me
mine only wayking [th]oughtslaughter
but today i survived i survived ? a lone i

   left the heat the cold for rain
i kissed a borrowed pug outside on the
payvehement wrote this instead
 of climbing in front
   the Train
&knocking loose my head

-less seed -less greed
i've a couple hours before
Death&i dream ourselves
the c/ageless sing

VII.

walk oh Howe !  we walk
    past chip bags turned over ovens coffee cups
      salt & vinegar & matcha latte & frozen yogurt sample spoons
    Siggi's gimmick weeds some empty sacks hyperloop around the carbon farming
     milkthistle & elm saplings

    butterfly breaks out
     of what obviously its own
     handmade body
   the pastskin not luminous at all
    wings flap a few times in sun

   light we Let it crawl
    from the plastic
      cashew container
   it climbs [anxious/envied/low/coral]

      -barely over between grass blades
   THEN &ONLY THEN onto a sprig ? of lavender? next!
    the slender pigweed
  Death's Garden
        They leave inside to do laundry

  i sit in the grass
    cross-legged [s]unbur[néd]
        - ning
   subtract the idea of progress   ooo
 nnnn    nnn    ooo ooo   nnn
   n       o         o       n
   ooo n nnn       nnn  oooo

singing a lullaby NO
not a lullaby not an Aubade not a Matin
not a[pp]Laud ? What is the Opposite    BEING
what IS the Opposite    OF SOUND
O PPO SITE O HMO O WHAT will?    BODY
AND
Charge me&Death the least    MIND
for the surgeries   we need   the hormones    DO HEREBY
for at least a year & a letter & other letters Dr.s    DE CLAIR DE
Notes so to the butterfly i sing the waking song coo calm    LUNATIC DE
i need help going    CROIRE à LEUR BONHEUR

to wake & Death needs help going to sleep
i practice on the butterfly the Manelied
meaning *hello & tomorrow*
terrifying white dots
cover its body

the clouds come
then the rain
then sleep
the sleep of green tomatoes
the long breath of St. John's Wort
&Ox-eye daisies& of Death
And of Death:

they can braid my hair. How she pulls it to... the decoratio
Made to feel so beautiful! i cannot say all that might mean.
builds a wood fire under the clawfoot bathtub he and othe
dragged out into the yard. Part of a wood stove for heatin
an old... oxidized like the earth up here in the
Pennsylvania mountains is how the tub grows hot, stays that w
A hose runs from the house to a gap where the faucet might go
extends up... the ushers... Feels as tall as Glenn does
times, it... wooden... that keeps the tub fro
burning... day. And i did ha
some wi... in the yard. i gue
got soaked and cold. Now the water almost too-hot to bear. A asks me if i w
a beer? I... put so much happiness in their eyes an
a smile? A... kinda like that but doesn't answer the questi
He brings... a Modelo, opened, with some lime. i don't know when he s
"...to hear about... when you were C's student. And now you're family." The sky is aln
all branches... C and i go for a hike. They point out these bright orange lizards. Say
to step on... not to contain my joy or excitement. What could i say about be
in the woods where i belong? Like hearing the way their feet fall on the rocky soil
see how the... boulder in the creek, aslant and full of cherishing. Near-wi
Once, on a... look. A had walked by and they were looking at his
Death brings ove... out of a transparent vacuum-sealed bag. The white sp
wrapping, between a painted pink canvas and little off-green alien figurines. An ora
book or a book painted orange. i still feel her calloused feet on my legs, her—i shouldn't say.
razor blade glued a terrible white streak on the pink canvas. What am I forgetting? The who
it. Three feet by two? Months pass and it falls from the hanging hook. We have broken up and
learning to love her in a different way i don't know how exactly yet. i finally read the words on the little wo
block that looks like it might should be on the wall at my mom's house: Do not walk behind me, i may not lead
not walk before me, i may not follow. Just walk beside me, and be my friend. For whatever reason, i though
text on the block was illegible? Or that it was some irony beyond me. Never did i consider that a quote people k
misattribute to Albert Camus would have the candor and breath i was aching for in our romance. Now it is the spring p
fall where every leaf is a flower, and the wind. They ask me after a while of not talking—with the rustling hair sliding bet
open fingers feels like she is cradling my head and a nylon string is open singing in my collarbone. i put my palms on the
stretching my fingers their tendons i feel in my elbows the taut grimace till it hurts a bit right where they connect. steadying my he
his fingers' motions in the strands, pulling tighter and softer to the end—How are you feeling—[So Good] or [Exhale, then]—What I
energy do you have, their voice is somehow expectant yet open, freeing—[i feel capable, yeah of anything you want to do]. i don't want to pr
them or make them feel like all i have been able to think about for weeks is playing a full scene with them—more hyperbole, i know. What am I allo
say? i am a girl not so practiced in fantasy or future, having any moments of potential and possibility yet tangible feels immense and expansive. W
continues, i am already reeling, swept up in the sensation their voice a warm fall somehow rain a quiet quieting enrapturing thing—Are you interested in what
about? How should i say? Yes, trying to not hide my exhilaration but also not sounding exasperated or desperate trying to live in the near moment and their han...

back at the bar bathroom i tend
the key stripped the loch
the loch stripped the key

we all thought the sea[l/t]
would be stuck forever

on who's chins/trap/on
i soapbox cry little transgirl tears
boohoo? are they talking about

This Guy Said His Partner [Death]
Is An Elementary School Teacher
Loves to Be Alive    Be Alive
Can You Believe That This Guy
This Guy Loves To Be Alive
This Guy   Be A live
This Guy

and[meaning true] i like to be included
in the conversation  so ? so? so i don't
let them know how wrong they are

i've gone where the wist is yrs
twelve days of who called?      BACK TO WORK
NO MSG receiving NO MSG receiving  oops! [is] a memory
No deluge? gotdamncallander cross'twires [c/t]rypt[ich!/o currency!]

o momen't fool

Deadloan i take His cat downstairs
in my arms
i take Her hand
i take Their waist
And Grow No Garden

ngertip is this a clamoring, Sir. Some glottal chrysalis? 'I'v
riends holding hands stand in front of me, the song thrummi
rom their necks. Stretched cloudscapes ache over the horiz
n the canvas-curtains, a horizon twenty feet tall. Sudden
he shift to Glenn's eyes enlarged to the size of your head, 
entire face returns to us. i have never seen a performer crea
a love song like this, with the whole body.    They remove
white-handled something like a molten foam under their b
she's going to beat me with that? No! let fear flit somewhe
n my face? i try to put generosity and grace there the wa
think Glenn shapes care and love in me. They sigh, "Alrea
n your knees?" i say i want the prayer to work. He has a sm
ut i am unsure, wearing little black swimshorts—the floor
old, but it takes some of the pain from my still-healing ank
My kneeling pooling cutting my circulation close. They begin
winnd this plastic sheen around my chest and arms as i mig
or a sofa or fridge to move up the stairs. My palms togeth
humbs to my sternum, elbows to my sides. He holds the end
my shoulder and pulls on the straining handle. A sensati
can't say, my skin losing contact with the air. They pull it t
nd connect the loose end to the newly wrapping wrappin
think it takes a few tries. i comply tonight because already 
ate and though it would be So Fun to get bratty, especially w
my ankles burning dulling, i want to show my respect for th
raft, our craft, and indulge my subservience. And i want

it rash it
i try i try i

mentuplets  hydra terr or wate®!
four-leaf Adonis
Mr. Persephone i look into
the water and it is
all you

've everknown   no one
kisses you

like a godde

no one knows how    Weare!

Ready to Die & so ready
to live   Swelt welts
All my affairs
In  Are   ORDER        UP
                    IT
oops at the bEAR bar BACK
forgetting where i'm supposed to be
where i'm expected
so howdy spell weather?

[Yarrow] it's roger from Whole Foods. Could you let me know if you quit or if something is wrong with you? I've been trying to reach you and I would just like confirmation if you are quitting or something happened to you.

*

saying makes difference. what kind how much depends on the time on the light bouncing of an eye little lazy one. drupe fist. like that. in the dream i asked the person to skin me alive. then they did. half-sleeve red but no blood on the floor. completely contained. made of crowbar made of flower patch some exhaust.

*

thanks for checking in. it's a word but i mean it's not too close. i think we'll be ok. the goblin witch behind the desk smiled at me. i mean ghosts are physical the way a voice and a recording of the voice is. my parents hit me a little but its sound pulls me apart. forceps red circle around my wrist. skin strips skin strips. in the dream i say I Love You but it doesn't feel any different.

*

Hi [Author's Name], I'm reaching out to follow-up about not reporting to your shift Sunday, (May 13th), from 9:30 to 12:30. We want to make sure that you are okay and touch base about this shift. We have not received any communication from you including a response to a voicemail and text messages we left for you on (Sunday May 13th). We hope all is well, and please reach out as soon as possible. Thank you!

81

no goblins here but plenty of other witches. the one offering tea samples in small cups. the orange one digging in my ear to make me hear again in stereo. now i am asked where that sound is coming from. i have to answer. wailing. my father drags chains locks and paper plates in the crawl space. asking someone if they're happy doesn't work. pressure i push the wax around with muscles i didn't know i had.

*

contract terminated. no ties. to this body. we, very unreasonably, have been held. after __ minutes of vibrating i go limp. the electricity still pulses hot cold to extremities. call a hand *tuning fork* to call myself *instrument*. cant open mouth. plugged up. wetness to make the current. two fingers i suck into my throat. to pass the wall outlet and not insert the key. call this success. a small victory. a thumb in a thimble thumb in a light socket. jigsaw puzzles everywhere i look want to be whole. so wet the piece won't fit.

*

make slippery. glint glance cannery. they found one bedbug on the couch. infestation or obsession or hyperbole or addiction. sprayed the whole apartment. care and abuse so often share a space so close, whether or not things are personal. dryer dryer. high heat and a bite. moon shudders through branches off the house next door. *so close oh* (so) *baby*('s ok but not surgeon or boilermaker or wainwright?) *that's gonna make me cum all over your face.* y'all or use.

ye is a form of yes. the plural. You the formal. for superiors. i wear a form of
address so others use the words i want them to. training or brainwashing i ring
the bell when i want this southern magnolia witch to take my orders i fuck in
the bathroom stall because i want to get fucked in the bathroom stall at a bar
so i can tell my friend the witch about it proof that i am gay & that i like boys
i fuck in the bathroom stall to prove myself to get a ri[s/m]e out of me but he
doesn't even pull my hair or rim me first or slap my ass rhizomatically.

*

[Yarrow], Are you ok? Can you give me a heads up on when you are working?
I think you missed a couple shifts but I'm not sure because things were moved
a round.

*

two spaces for a long pause. James says *wow he must be really into you*. if i call
u a wolf will u show me yr teeth. dirk asks me to reimagine the grandmother
in little red riding hood as a transwoman. oh what an entsetztlich (to put out
as an adverb) large muzzle you have! all the better (orig. fressen) to eat you
(imp. like an animal) with. appallingly. the fairytale romance isn't over it never
happened. no morals. *where definitely going to hell* on the first night. repeat
someone's name five times to imprint it. try a hundred with their hand in
you(rs). part of taming. to subject use thou instead of thee. nominally. when i
open my eyes sometimes a wolf sometimes a hunter sometimes i am pulled
from a cavity because? no lesson. except maybe. how deep & how loud.

ave said something similar. But i have felt my sweetheart Patience, rea
nder my hair and with two fingers loosen every knot. Then, too, i ha
vanted desperately to bawl. Sometimes, i do, when she offers that

a solar system    without borders    my lovers my noon-
less sun

ne, when teething soft or slowly, teasingly excavating into. Sometime
annot. And she understands this is what it is to be cursed. And sometim

close  ing  cloud  hor[rid/izon/rere/mone y]  backwash

ve share in that curse. And sometimes our hands and our mouths f
he counterspells.    i think i should tell a story about my grandmoth

smaller tallow  wedged   green-black body becoming Lake
we never talked

er 90-year old new beau R, my gr...    i wonder if i ca

swim lessons    i tire treading so fast

vant to tell you the way Glenn and Elizabeth tell each other what they
n the silent scene. Things they have told each other time and again. Wh

i don't float even when i'm alive
no matter how big these tits get

lits between their fingers... i say i want
The Estrogen Papers say Your fat will be redistributed

ell you a story about my grandma Louie. i mean one time my sweethe
f ten years and i arrive at her house. we pull up alongside the row of p

[s]ample    bloodwork
tells me the truth
in advertising:

rees in the backyard. The driveway curves up and you can feel it in yo
hins coming up to the porch. My father, her son, killed himself abou
month before. Why did i mention that? She poured me a cup of coffee a
ve had yet to sit down. She says, "The other morning, i just couldn't
myself up out of bed. i had bowling that afternoon and plans with Ral
just couldn't do it. Your father—i just cried the whole morning. Ral
alled me. i said, 'i don't know, Ralph. i'm just so sad. i can't today.' He t
ne, 'Well, Louie, that's ok. i think you oughta go to your bathroom, tak
hower, put your makeup on, and get yourself fixed up. And you can st
our day and you'll start to feel a whole lot better. How bout that?'" A
here is some silence. My sweetheart says that often helps them, i gue
eems kinda obvious what's helpful and unhelpful about it. But t
alph was sweet to call. And we talk some more. Abruptly as the st
arted, my gram says, "But i never did get out of bed that day. i was f
he next. But that day i never even opened the blinds." Then she says, "Y
now that pot i had setting out right here with nothing growing in it bu
unch of little weeds? i decided to clean it out, and in it i had a whole m
f sweet potatoes, just right like that." Her hands kinda like you wo
antomime binoculars, but staggered so they fit like puzzle pieces. T

[ you are wanted!! you are wanted
    for what
you grab off the shelf – [a]naphora [b]anal, [c]ant
    you are worth
What YOU?! [goods  ] – new line station
        [ byes ]
                        ]
the water sings clacking branches leaves the blood
        in my coffee cup   a swallow
Deathslapping my face
    eroding my freckles
        & their legends of burns

        in midsummer now it is
    thunderlapping on the shore
of my waist      belly scarred X to double up X

            Y-Death is wanted
                for what good
        [?] till the last drop
            Death is worth
        the last inch of topsoil

ng together, maybe." "So cooked that up yesterday. Had Ralph over for dinner.
en i climb on top of him in his cramped front seat, i am already trembling. This
ws. i hope what they release in me, what pours out as i straddle and thread my
ckles through the thick skin you can use. Is something you
e wanted. Is something you might cherish, longing and wonder—if we might
r touch, if we might even ourselves in these moments, if we might feel more
y alive, if we might soothe the ... dening and the vulnerabilities scraped into
So when there is more breath in me and i look into their eyes, it is cave and it is
ne-lit and hillock stream... it knows about ... ing sky and gold-flecked glutton
rise above an ancient ... living... There is a heron, plummeting, a sense of if—
it been knocked from flight or fell—already through the haze, but this was in
Pennsylvania mountains where my friend shows me their morning fishing spot
nming that Glenn tune. "Welcome the spring and summer rain / Softly turned
ing again. / Welcome ... now, we are ne-ver new." The force, it's like
sper, it's like a shushing, when he says "Softly" and the urgency of it. A has tha
d of whisper. And two dogs appear, just in front of a man who walks by with a
on his hip. He says, "Oh! They're ... but my friend was anxious about the
ol and the bullets. As i hold you now, my body as i held you then as i have tried
old myself and let feeling first course, sweeping into ground into water, and a
d become the eternal river, bubbling over the poured rock. i try to place my hand
ne crucifix of our neck. And i learn, and i pray over the knots of their shoulders
eading and folding and unraveling as tender as i can, as deep as i can reach, the
k, healing not-yet scars stretching across chest to armpits. And tell me, certai
ds of pulling (toward your spine) stretch and hurt the healing tissue. So i pull from
top of the spine at the top of the neck with all the force i can offer. To dig steadily
ween the roots and the way one must  move and breathe and gasp reminds me o
elf in Death's Patient everstrong hands. Stopping begging. Stopping when i can
athe through it. The difference between feeling pain and holding it and letting i
s through you, rather than taking it and not feeling it at all, and this is the struggl
ur touch but That's It, as we breathe out together in one. So there's no reason fo
o pretend my toes aren't dancing in my workboots, that i am not soaked through

coda

Death&i decide not to live together
Walking gets harder     thank moss i need

i let the program take control the text writer
The keyboard app on my phone says begin large

End small into a dot red lines under score me
Tally me chalk me up cover me in yr dust

I hit thi spici kiy with bith thimbs to ilign
43 times? Trying enact my desires over my

Constraints as usual as rveryone does
So i give myself up but not up like What's Up Like

space    i have trouble describing
The sunrise over the Lake

Like: televangelist gold bright   nuclear waste
M   cantalope   watermelon     hybrid
Waking up after ectomy       sirgery   Death rubs yr shoulders
Sponges left after soaking       xzvpβoine qpdfo≠ivadf¥vna apirŒihiht Bent
Colony of lovers kissing on canvas
beach towels       & teeth     Death   brewsows
                                              mead
tribbingly      delirious     ripe
avocados in the dumpster outside       the store  the anthill  under
rock              accidental belly-flopt
who    callous     coffee to liquor
back and forth repeat repeat
first clean drink of water
God     someone  recognizes you
You recognize yrself
&you are happy to see Them in you

Mercy licks the only drop O Great
Mystery each lash leaves me    hol[  ]
   (a small valley between mounthains)

sick with grief, a splitting
      whisper     the fear doesn't come
      without imagination. Neither do i why

         i swallow the hair my hair
darning  in the water  the breath bubbles
      through Little Geyser    (what forms)

      feature [     snag a lip]  i invent
songs for the puncture   Dirges
         for what welts    (a word for pulsate

      worlds)   hunk of. Leaving the
leaving happens before i feel presence
      pomegranating The skin

      denatures. Does the weeping echo?  Is she herself
         the echo?    Are you a willow? Do you see
      any blue?

Because I am forced to look for vengeance in a pink coral circle

Because my nails bend split in half like a candy wrapper

Because you deserve more than

Because

Because five were taken and I do not know one man who can atone for even one life alone

Because there is only liberation and it is a river

Because it is cut into canals and dams and reverse and spoiled and deemed unsafe to swim in

Because I swim in it and press my lips to it and suck the water from the surface and carry buckets of it to boil and filter

Because a sip will not suffice

Because you deserve more than

Because every day more are taken from us

Because every day more must lie in wait

Because the only damage i deserve is a requisite mouth and begged-for blade and your pleasure

Because there is all the time in the world

Because there is very little

Because you deserve so much more than

Because

Because there is no sacred game more powerful

Because there is only a river

Because the river begins as several and ends as several

Because it does begin

Because it does not end

Because it does not end like this

# Maid Notes

i arrive to my client's house. i start with the dishes. i forget to check the two-tiered drying rack box called a dishwasher. i am tired the 50 minutes to bike here. i do not sit down.

i stand at the sink and play Youtube or Pennsound available lectures. Fred Moten says "Implicit in all this is that the consent not to be a single being is at once essential to and in excess of any poetics of relation."

The family does not use sponges or warshcloths for the dishes. There is one in the bathroom. Scrubbing plastic brushes, i assume, i use those for the stove. i take the sponge to the sink.

Pour-over coffee pot catfood dishes ceramic plates light forks spoons butter knives rarely a sharp one. The rice cooker usually has dry not-moldy rice in it.

The cast iron "combo" cooker on the stove has some oil. Nearby, a large pot of kernels and burnt butter.

i scour. i never wear gloves. Steel wool. Rearrange my fingerprints.

i switch hands then start on the stove, the greasy also kernelly. i think, "I wish my wrists were more flexible." i try to come up with a new adage: "Can't wash dishes in a dirty sink," or, maybe, "a sponge has many mouths but no tongue." i work on this book when i give myself, generously, a coffee break.

*Death and* is a struggle to work with. It requires confronting two coping mechanisms that i've realized have stopped serving me to the extent that i would like: 1. (intrusive) suicidal ideation 2. unhealthy attachment to/idealization of a loved one. What once helped me to survive a long period of twenty or so years of dysphoria, dysmorphia, abuse, and neglect became natural reactions to minimal stress: overworking, depression, mania, reading, or having an unoccupied moment of free-time. i often replaced one obsession with the other—that i might switch from plotting, witnessing, and reliving my own death to instead imagining every moment a loved one was living.

Tonight i will take a walk. Someone jumps out from behind a bush to slash my throat. i don't see the person—it's the flash of blade off the streetlight. No. i imagined it again. Heartbeat in my ears and mouth, can't hear Joanna Newsom sing, "It does not suffice, to merely lie beside each other, as those who love each other do." Follow a daydream of my sibling playing a game we used to share called *Darkest Dungeon*.

Or, i here i am driving my van and fantasizing about drowning myself in Lake Michigan. Then switch to listing why i want to live some more: Biz and i hide in the bathtub on New Year's Eve and they make me laugh about the Wikipedia page for magenta; Matthias holds me up in the ocean at the queer beach, kissing me through the brine gushing out of our mouths. Back to: Throwing myself out a window.

Always somewhere already, a visual first: i am flayed alive, my skin is on a table, electrocuted by placing my key in a wall outlet, stepping off the roof at a reading for my friend's book release. &c &c &c. It could last all day—through teaching my composition classes, talking to a customer at the bar, having sex, performing.

i should say i know this is not entirely uncommon. Less rare than being Trans- anyway. But who knows for sure. Having said too much as usual, i mean to bring this up for purpose of relating obsessive thinking patterns to the construction and methods of this text.

Is it in part from a refusal of my own perversions? To have hidden them beneath other horrors and other identities and other desires in favor of those somehow more palatable? If I look closely, the story is all there.

Scrub awhile, then spray the cleaning solution to soak into what's left. A lot. The cabinet tops, the ceiling fan, the cookbooks, and the rest are coated in oil-dust. Turn it off, remove the loose pages and for some reason several needles and syringes from the hanging shelf greased. i use wood-cleaner polish rub down the walls baseboards. Move appliances and flour containers from one counter to a chair. "Words do not always do what they say," Sara Ahmed writes in "An Affinity of Hammers."

i scrub and sing *Chip Chip Chip*
  *cracking paint or cracking wall*
  *don't let me forget*
  *the hammering is camouflage*

The singing does some work on its own, the concentrated circulation and recirculation of bleach and vinegar. Other cleaning chemicals my alveoli harbor for some time.

Cleaning is a healing practice. To be intimate with a space. Localized sterilization. Down the drain, the estrogen i inject i piss out.

"You gotta learn to not complain," sings the man on the Christian radio station, then the living room must be dusted.

i might take the dog Mr. Darcy out. Should i have pulled the oven and dishwasher away to sweep? i'll do that.

the first time i worked as a cleaner for this person, she said *I Don't Want to Exploit Your Labor,* then brought me a coffee.

Reciprocal the nail and the hammer.

i tear a knuckle wide open on a sharp edge of a counter.

i do not say CUNT in exasperation, though i admire its tenacity as an expletive over the centuries— feels nostalgic. Rather, i say COCK,

but i realize the problem happens to be my client is home sick, and hearing your transwoman maid yell "CAWWWWck!" whether or not it follows a thud and gasp, might be disturbing.

i write *Death and* by hand: with a pen and a small notebook. On the way to and from work, if i take mass transit, sometimes on breaks, the only spare time i can find. i mention this because my hands cramp up something fierce after a couple lines. Then, in transcribing this work into a rudimentary word processor on my phone (my laptop died), every tiny move is excruciatingly difficult to translate into the program.

A lowercase singular first-person pronoun (i) requires deleting the autocorrected text (I) three times before the program relents. That is the easiest fix. Multiple spaces between words, within a word, capitalizing an individual letter, or misspelling, kennings, &c. were almost impossible. Copying and pasting for rearrangement can take an hour for one page.

The least of it. i have to fight the program, the natural order of text, for even a tiny trespassing (as we forgive those), let alone superimposition or other textual malformities. But i am a malaphor[m] of this moment—so too must be the work. Each little transgression necessitated an obsessive insistence on tapping the space key exactly 14 times per line or introducing a stable subscript. i think this text tries to redefine naturalized orders and sequences. Mine and others placed next to me. Wrapped around me. Ones i learned. Others i invented.

But now there is blood i must wipe off the side of the cat litter container home object. Now the thick smell catpiss and the litter in the blood soaking, i am thinking i should say something about bodily fluids and disgust.

Now this is a micro essay about Samuel Delaney and the power of disturbance, however no. Not now: "the point of the pointed foot also served as a brief tangent between contact and leap" (Ryoko Sekiguchi, from *Heliotropes*). My friend says, "Dancing teaches you how to love your body." Or, that's a paraphrase in response to the quote from *Pride and Prejudice*: "To be fond of dancing was a certain step toward falling in love." But my lover learned how to hate his Trans body through ballet. Unlearning now through ballet and dance what it originally taught him. Unlearning all of us:

A floor can be painted to look like wood. Or to hide the wood beneath. A thin spill of cement. Can cover then be uncovered. It might crack, you can use something thick. To fill them. Oops

i have stood how long looking at the ink on my arm. Redouble fits, but i don't trust it. So onto the bookshelves with knickknacks, a tiny sand and stone garden thing, dust collectors.

Do i feel empty because i have no photos in my room? Or that all the work i do feels like tithing. Someone i will shake hands with has passed me a collection plate. i place an envelope therein. i turn the oven on to CLEAN. The envelope catches fire. Then the forest. Where a hand appraises a surface feeling for anomalies.

The couch must be lifted to clean, then i think, "How long to linger on someone's lips?"

Bleach has long been used to as a disinfectant, you can but should not (a friend tells me) use it for undrinkable water when boiling is not an option. Some nurses still use it in a pinch—according to online forums—many homesteaders use it as a treatment for poison ivy.

The handheld vacuum cleaner can reach dog toys, shoulder work. i feel strong doing the work my mother did, same as when i cut my own bangs. i grew up in her home/basement salon. i swept the hair and refilled the blue liquid after dumping it on the driveway. Run off, now i empty the tiny receptacle into a larger one. The recycling

is full. All three. Doesn't matter from what i hear.

It all goes to the same home for abandoned toys.

The cleaning solution should have done something to the stove by now.

i hate transactions—that someone tells me "Put it down your throat," and pays me an agreed upon amount and i do. The program calls this a "Tip," like a suggestion. The suggestion of a balanced equation, of a perfect ratio. i'll help you move, and you let me ask you question about how you fell in love. Healing cannot be a transaction, but it so often is. i'm not sure if that can be true:

At equilibrium in a chemical reaction, this does not mean it has stopped moving. That it is dead. Forward and reverse reactions occur at the same rate. Baking soda and vinegar when i'm at home. But here

i use a product with dipotassium carbonate and ethanolamine. There isn't anything interesting to say about those two chemicals. Except, maybe that ethanolamine can be used as a carbon scrubber in air (filtration) systems such as in submarines or spacecraft. This is a healing of the earth, an environment. A small thing like a yellow flower known as a weed. Perhaps this ability to dissolve carbon is why it's in this product.

i scrub with my right arm until it burns. i switch arms, but my left can't do a circular motion, so i have to be linear with my movements. i want to try to be fair. In the film i'm "watching" now [because Fred Moten is too beautiful to follow along with when i'm scrubbing], she says, "this is to show you how much easier life is when there are two instead of one," and she handcuffs his right hand behind his back.

The cramps come easy. Meaning bent or crooked. i take a break and scrub the toilet with its shit stains and cranky angles. i pour bleach and scrub with a sponge. i don't wear gloves. i tell my friend, "i think they get in the way." Particles swirl around my finger, the one with the fresh wound. i take a photo on my knees and send it to someone. When i am bound, i say "Thank you," and "Please," and "Are you even trying? It's cute." "This land of thorns is not habitable," Gloria Anzuldua wrote in a book (*This Bridge Called My Back*) a friend lent me, which i think of now because, well i'm not sure i guess.

Because i care for them and they care for me. Or, that i wish i knew how to care for them better, because they care for me so well. And all of my sisters, and brothers.

i use two hands—one to apply pressure and one to direct it. The book, i think, is about unity. Not selling. Although the book i read to a room of people last night was about presenting a storefront display. "Think of how much money you will save!" It said several times. Or seemed to.

Sometimes i am asked to draw blood. And this too, is an act of healing. Or, rather, i believe most acts with the right attention can be healing. But others are specifically suited for it. The separation of skin, for instance. For a moment. i don't mean to be medieval. Cold water then sea salt is how i get blood out of my clothes.

i have never once been tipped while working as a maid. In another type of work i do, all of my money is Tips. i might have said this already. Sometimes i pretend to choke. Other times i pretend i am not choking. Careful to not ruin a voice. i make circles on the stove. To turn, as on a lathe. These are ways to make people feel good. When my kitty comes home from the shelter with me, he sounds scared, hoarse in his small cardboard box carrier, so i sing to him: *Foxglove an alley cuss, loves his dirt and a midnight hush...*

Now he wanders around my apartment and sings loudly. When he enters a room. Midday or 4 am. *Mow-WoWW? Mowohng.* The stove is coming along. i cheat sometimes and use a fork or a hard metal object to scrape up the bits. But you have to take care. It can plow right through the enamel. i might use my nails, but the carbon sticks sharp into my quick. And then the rust begins.

The people who hire me, hire me to make them feel safe. Safe enough to come. Safe enough to use their home. The suggestion: here, and now, no one can consent properly or indefinitely. A moment. To refuse to relate? Or exist without and how to get further from. To quarantine. To deny a piece of the whole. To accept. Maybe.

Meg Day has an enlightening and challenging poem (and titular chapbook), "When all you have is a hammer," that in part, directs us toward the beauty and purpose of betweenity and fluidity and away from Conclusion or Completion or Product as a desired/possible/useful space. i think Conclusions and Completions and Products served humanity for a long time, in many wonderful and many more terrible ways—hoping we can put them aside until we can use them more lovingly.

i too have been trying to discard the tools that were once useful but are no longer. Or at least put them back on the shelf when i'm done. All healing can become poison, for the healer and the healed. i think i am learning. i can clean twice a week before my throat starts to burn. i know how to dig the crust out from under my nails with my sharp little teeth.

Notes

## Canto I.

My misquoting of "Sleep, those little slices of death—how I loathe them" is from *Nightmare on Elm Street 3: Dream Warriors* (1987). In the film it is misattributed to Edgar Allen Poe, but really it should be attributed to Wes Craven (plus Bruce Wagner, Frank Darabont, Chuck Russell), who invented the phrase and the genius idea to attach Poe to it, and who at this point may hold as much literary weight as The Father of the Modern Detective Story? Anyway, according to interviews, the film originated with the idea that it would follow children/adolescents to a specific location to commit suicide, eventually revealed to be led by The Springwood Slasher. The actual film follows suicide and self-harm in a different way, in that Mr. Krueger's (whose name is a veraltete German word that means Innkeeper/barkeep) attacks in the teenagers' hospital are regarded as suicide attempts/cutting/ addiction/etc. The recurrent trauma is misunderstood by those in power, whose work on the victims/patients makes them ultimately more susceptible to Freddy.

To talk a little further about the relationship between the work i've done as a bartender (at a grocery store)/sex worker/housemaid/dogwalker is intimately connected (for me) with healing: making someone a cocktail, something to nourish them, asking them about their day/life/ problems and usurping the work done for tips to treat the soda drinker with the same respect and courtesy as the fancy cocktail boy at the bar, is in the same realm as sending my transDad a poem I think he might like; handling a stranger's body as a lover might (not to say Johns are not on a spectrum from total piece of garbage to at least courteous to strange angels), usually followed by a precious afterglow of tending to their emotional needs in the same way, is akin to a homemade wedding gift, cleaning someone's home, making their space more comfortable and livable is as tender and affectionate as rubbing my lover's shoulders when they get off work. &c &c &c. Of course, navigating these positions require different methods of keeping myself safe, and different levels and means of protection. A bag for bodily fluids. Gloves. And, of course, I need to get paid. Is healing possible under & within our current socio-economic structures? And what kinds? And what does it mean to restore?

When I really need to pay rent, pay my medical debt, buy gas, there's a toxicity, a creeping, obvious, terrible inauthenticity to the transaction. This feels related, too, to loving my people. When I feel most in need of affection, I feel least capable of giving it, not without that incessant, imminent, and dangerous mistreatment. Misquoting Poe? Propagating it with some Hollywood Magic and a Booming Box Office. Misinterpreting the effects of Krueger's razor on a wrist.

The Rosmarie Waldrop line "Once you blur the distinction between equal and equivocal, space is interrupted and disappears in subcutaneous shivers," comes from *Lawn of Excluded Middle*, part two "The Attraction of Falling," the section/poem titled "Mass, Momentum, Stress."

The TC Tolbert line ("tonight let's practice erosion / it's finally my turn as the wind") is from a book very dear to me, *Gephyromania*, though i'm seeing it's also a part of a chapbook *territories of folding*.

 "I will live in thy heart, die in thy lap, and be buried in thy eyes; and moreover, I will go with thee to thy uncle's." So says Benedick in *Much Ado About Nothing* right after he says he is a bad poet. Sorry Beatrice: "I cannot show it in rhyme. I have tried. I can find out no rhyme to "lady" but "baby"—an innocent rhyme...No, I was not born under a rhyming planet, nor I cannot woo in festival terms."

For the life of my i cannot find a source in which the villain-man threatens the hero's love interest, "I can make you laugh," but i know it's on one of the thousand or so bootlegged VHS tapes at my childhood home. Could it be the Jack Nicholson version of the Joker? i don't think so. This piece happened with much gratitude to Tony Trigilio and his *Dark Shadows* work.


## Canto II.
"GREET EVERYONE WITHIN" is all found text taken from my orientation/indoctrination session at Whole Foods. Many thanks, by the way, to Harryette Mullen and *S\*PeRM\*\*K\*T* which may not be directly quoted or paraphrased here, but was necessary reading to me about a year before I began on *Death and*.

The Strokes and The Arctic Monkeys feature in "Happens: to be cleaned" because they were playing during the scene, but also because if there were an archetypical Sad Boy, it would be Julian Casablancas or Alex Turner. I imagine both of them having said—in their own lifetimes or in past ones—what that man on the CTA said to me, "You're too pretty to cry on the bus."

Damn. I spent a lot of time wishing that guy would have flown me down to N. Carolina.

Diatoms really do produce 20% of the oxygen on Earth. They die and people use them to kill bed bugs (and other insects), because diatoms are so sharp-bodied they cut them right up. When we had a bed bug scare, my housemates and i poured dead diatoms into plastic cups and placed legs of furniture in them. Little piles of bodies all of the apartment. It takes a corpse to make a corpse. Or, it takes a corpse to protect the living. Hm.

"from June 18" is a tribute to Joanne Kyger, and Bernadette Mayer. Without Joanne's *About Now*, without Bernadette's *Midwinter Day*, the epic daily love poem, *Death and* wouldn't exist. The same could be said of *The Pulp Vs. The Throne* by Carrie Lorig (thanks to Leslie, there isn't thanks enough) and *Kill Manual* by Cassandra Troyan (thanks Matthias, there isn't thanks enough). Laura Goldstein's *Safe Wars* and Bhanu Kapil's *Ban en Banlieue* and *Humanimal: A Project for Future Children* were also necessary while writing this.

"i am afrayd / i am riting myself / metonymic off deth" is from *feeld* by Jos Charles, with thanks to Noah for passing it onto me when I most needed it.

"Trying to Ctrl+Alt+Del / My [pussy/asshole]" is my own line, but it wouldn't exist without the talented Juliana Huxtable, whose *MUCUS IN MY PINEAL GLAND* will forever be close to my heart and the top of my recommendations.

Other books I was reading, relevant to "Is Trump still president[...]": *The Sexual Organs of The IRS* by Jennifer Karmin and Bernadette Mayer; *Carceral Capitalism* by Jackie Wang; *Normal Life* by Dean Spade; *Sad Girl Poems* by Christopher Loma Soto.

**Canto III.**
My dad did say he would hang himself once the money ran out.

"i left & met Death..." is in part thanks to Lisa Fishman's "Initialing" process. Briefly, an outline: attend to a voice (a song, recited poem, overheard conversation, commercial, &c) and write down the first letter of every word. As many as you can, anyway. From there, fill in the space following the first letter with more letters if you want, as fast as you can. From there, Poem? Sometimes. I do this often. This one worked. I wish I knew the original/inspiring text though. I think it was a recording of Mary Ruefle's "28 Short Lectures." I worked a lot to her readings at the time.

"The Beautiful Uncut hair of graves." Death quotes this to me often. It's from Walt Whitman's *Song of Myself*.

"Death dreams Death..." references the fact that mosquitos are in fact very important pollinators in many ecosystems. It also refers to the fact that only female mosquitos bite us, and this is for their children. Also "The Flea" by John Donne is a poem I have read.

i laughed a lot when writing this section/canto/poem. Wishing i were laughing with you right now.

i used to say "Quitting cigarettes is the hardest thing I ever chose to do." i'm so very lucky that is so far from the truth, now.

When my transDad said he was going to leave for [city far away], he proposed a pilgrimage to Bloomington to visit the community orchard where many poems as well as the titular poem in *Catalog of Unabashed Gratitude* find some setting in. Sitting on a kinda cold stone bench, nearer to one another than he and I have been in a long time, we listened to a reading of that poem and cried. i don't know why my Dad was crying. For my part, i felt the loss between us and before us and behind us. A loss in the silences in the years since we met and lost touch. A loss, it was too easy to think of. We disagreed on the way home, and there were hours of silence underneath the rock CD we bought at the thrift store. The night before, i mentioned how weird it was there wasn't a lock on the door to the home-share rental place. Not long after, a naked man barged into our room with his dick in his hand. He was red, sunburnt and drunk, before he noticed me, blurting, "Sorry, I thought this was the bathroom." He pulled the door and his towel shut. i kept thinking about that during Ross Gay's reading of the poem in the orchard the next day. Ross's writing, in particular that book, is essential to *Death &*. For that matter Aram Saroyan, and Douglas Kearney are too. As long as we're giving not enough credit where too much is due, CM Burroughs, W.S. Merwin, Hannah Wiener, Charles Bernstein, and n.h. pritchard too deserve very much. Thanks to the Eclipse Project Archive, also for all the easy access to strange, nearly lost writings.

### Canto IV.
"That thogh he hadde me bet on every bon, / he koude wynne agayn my love anon," "What thing is it that women moost desiren," and "I trowe I loved hym best for that he was of his love daungerous to me" come from The Wife of Bath's Prologue in *The Canterbury Tales*. The Wife of Bath has been read as a proto-feminist, because she is a woman who challenges social order and the misogynistic interpretation of scripture, who has herself "been the whippe," a dominatrix(?), or one who plies herself to a trade (what sounds like now a banal conception of economics of sex (work/within and without marriage), and who has sought her own sexual and marital partners. The question of "Sovereynetee" is predominant: Who has the right exercise desire and control? And how? At a time when rhyming was thought to build an inextricable bind between words and concepts, Chaucer rhymes "Sovereynetee" with "He." The Wife of Bath supposedly fails in her argument because she wields scripture interpretation against scripture interpretation. i put my lips against my lovers when we spat—if i'm lucky—gloss fights gloss.

"Call this something else. Last night it had a name, /a name wedged between an organ's teeth..." comes from the third stanza in Patricia Smith's "Prologue—And Then She Owns You" from *Blood Dazzler* and ends as follows "...a name pumping a virgin unawares, a curse word. / Wail it, regardless."

What kind of baby Transgirl would I be if I didn't quote Andrea Long Chu's "On Liking Women" (n+1, Issue 30)?" where i snagged the long quote. Chu reasons that desire has been wielded against Trans- to deny them these civil rights (i.e. saying one *wants* to be a woman means one is *not currently* a woman—transitioning is also a word suggestive of this claim—at one point one has not been a woman, at some point one will *become* a woman, thanks to medical technology, presentation, or other social maneuvering). A greeting card for the trans person in your life reads, "You are becoming who've you always been." Weird rephrasing of Heidegger's *immer schon*, or "always already." A woman at the bar I was tending, someone i could not discard myself from, asked me (after more than a year on HRT, at my work where my bosses used she pronouns), very hushed, "Oh, so do you want to be one of these transgenders?"

"i was never one body" is for/after Cody-Rose Clevidence.

### Canto V.-End
"[Yarrow], it's Roger from..." could not have existed without kari edwards, or for that matter Trace Peterson and her poems, especially *Since I Moved In. EOAGH* and its issues have also done much for this book, which is where I first encountered Julian Talamantez Brolaski's work, before I read the hilarious and brilliant Of *Mongrelitude* which somehow didn't make it into this text by means of quotation. Though paraphrase and allusion, I'm sure. This piece owes much to David Trinidad, his work, and the indescribable many things he shared with me.

Susan Howe and CA Conrad were also instrumental to this text. Alice Notley same, more and more. Thanks to Leslie for those four books of hers: *Songs for the Unborn Second Baby, Margaret & Dusty, At Night the States*. Oh my time of little gods, *At Night the States*. Thanks to Matthias for reading almost all of *Alma, Or, The Dead Woman* to me as a bedtime story.

I think "skin strips skin strips" is a reference/homage to a poem in Hoa Nguyen's *Violet Energy Ingots*, though most of my love poems are born out of her tradition and all the sweetheart lines in *Red Juice*.

### Coda
Wishing always to love you more.

## Acknowledgements

*Death and* took many forms and pieces over the last however long. Many of those pieces are available/forthcoming thanks to the wonderful people and editors at

*Dream Pop Press*
*E-Ratio*
*Scab*
*DREGINALD*
*Thin Noon*
*where is the river*
*a) glimpse) of)*
*The Twang Anthology*
*EOAGH*

www.ingramcontent.com/pod-product-compliance
Lightning Source LLC
Chambersburg PA
CBHW061149030426

42335CB00003B/157